Best Loved
POEMS
To Read
Again & Again

Best Loved
POEMS
To Read
Again & Again

The Most Moving Verses
in the
English Language

Compiled by
Mary Sanford Laurence

Galahad Books   **New York City**

*To Chantal, Jill,
Lynn, and Mark*

Copyright © 1979 by Hart Associates

This edition originally published in 2 volumes as POEMS THAT
STIR THE HEART and POEMS OF SENTIMENT AND INSPIRATION.

All rights reserved. No part of this work may be
reproduced or transmitted in any form or by any
means, electronic or mechanical, including photocopying,
recording, or any information storage and retrieval
system, without permission in writing from the
publisher.

Published in 1988 by
Galahad Books, a division of LDAP, Inc.
166 Fifth Avenue
New York, New York 10010

By arrangement with Hart Associates

Library of Congress Catalog Card Number: 86-81169
ISBN: 0-88365-714-7

Printed in the United States of America

Contents

CELEBRATION

FACING DEATH

FACING LIFE

FAITH

FATHERS

FRIENDSHIP

FULFILLMENT

GRIEF

MORTALITY

MOTHER

PATRIOTISM

PHILOSOPHY

REFLECTIONS

REMEMBRANCE

Foreword

Have you ever felt something so strongly that it seemed like ordinary words couldn't express your emotion? Perhaps you wanted to tell a friend how much you valued him, or maybe you wanted to give hope to someone who was caught in the clutches of the Giant Despair. Perhaps your heart was full with a sense of joy in nature, or with grief at the loss of a loved one.

In such moments, we often turn to poetry. Poetry satisfies our longing for beauty and for inspiration. Poetry cheers us when we're sad, or lonely. Poetry comforts us when we lose our loved ones, or feel nostalgia for the past. Poetry entertains us, moves us, strengthens us, gives voice to the thoughts that, as Wordsworth said, "do often lie too deep for tears." That's why, for thousand of years, poems have been written and read.

This collection of verses contains many of the favorite poems of the American people. Here are poems about brotherhood, desire, courage, and love. Here are poems of celebration, of inspiration, of thankfulness; poems to renew our faith in God and in human goodness; poems to help us have patience in times of trial, and poems to tell those closest to us how much they mean to us. This is not an anthology of academic poems for scholars, but a selection of verses that have touched and stirred the hearts of millions of ordinary human beings for many years. Here are poems by Alfred Tennyson and Edgar Guest, Christina Rossetti and Margaret E. Sangster, and many other poets. Some of the poets in this volume are well-known; some are not so well known. But all of them had the ability to express the deep emotions that come to everyone, to give words to the various moods, feelings, and thoughts that are a part of our human make-up. Here are poems to read and reread, whenever we are deeply moved.

Best Loved
POEMS
To Read
Again & Again

At Nightfall

I need so much the quiet of your love
 After the day's loud strife;
I need your calm all other things above
 After the stress of life.

I crave the haven that in your dear heart lies,
 After all toil is done;
I need the starshine of your heavenly eyes,
 After the day's great sun.

CHARLES HANSON TOWNE

Love's Philosophy

The fountains mingle with the river,
    And the rivers with the ocean;
The winds of heaven mix forever,
    With a sweet emotion;
Nothing in the world is single;
    All things by a law divine
In one another's being mingle:—
    Why not I with thine?

See! the mountains kiss high heaven,
    And the waves clasp one another;
No sister flower would be forgiven
    If it disdained its brother;
And the sunlight clasps the earth,
    And the moonbeams kiss the sea:—
What are all these kissings worth,
    If thou kiss not me?

PERCY BYSSHE SHELLEY

Death, Be Not Proud

Death, be not proud, though some have called thee
    Mighty and dreadful, for thou art not so;
    For those whom thou think'st thou dost overthrow
Die not, poor Death, nor yet canst thou kill me.
From rest and sleep, which but thy pictures be,
    Much pleasure; then from thee much more must flow,
And soonest our best men with thee do go,
Rest of their bones, and soul's delivery.

Thou art slave to fate, chance, kings, and desperate men,
    And dost with poison, war, and sickness dwell;
    And poppy or charms can make us sleep as well
And better than thy stroke; why swell'st thou then?
    One short sleep past, we wake eternally,
    And death shall be no more; Death, thou shalt die.

JOHN DONNE

Requiescat

Strew on her roses, roses,
    And never a spray of yew:
In quiet she reposes;
    Ah, would that I did too!

Her mirth the world required;
    She bathed it in smiles of glee.
But her heart was tired, tired,
    And now they let her be.

Her life was turning, turning,
    In mazes of heat and sound.
But for peace her soul was yearning,
    And now peace laps her round.

Her cabined, ample spirit,
    It fluttered and failed for breath;
Tonight it doth inherit
    The vasty hall of death.

MATTHEW ARNOLD

The Stone

"And you will cut a stone for him,
To set above his head?
And will you cut a stone for him—
A stone for him?" she said.

Three days before, a splintered rock
Had struck her lover dead—
Had struck him in the quarry dead,
Where, careless of the warning call,
He loitered, while the shot was fired—
A lively stripling, brave and tall,
And sure of all his heart desired. . .
A flash, a shock,
A rumbing fall. . .
And, broken 'neath the broken rock,
A lifeless heap, with face of clay;
And still as any stone he lay,
With eyes that saw the end of all.

I went to break the news to her;
And I could hear my own heart beat
With dread of what my lips might say
But, some poor fool had sped before;
And flinging wide her father's door,

Had blurted out the news to her,
Had struck her lover dead for her,
Had struck the girl's heart dead in her,
Had struck life lifeless at a word,
And dropped it at her feet:
Then hurried on his witless way,
Scarce knowing she had heard.

And when I came, she stood alone,
A woman turned to stone:
And, though no word at all she said,
I knew that all was known.
Because her heart was dead,
She did not sigh nor moan,
His mother wept;
She could not weep.
Her lover slept:
She could not sleep.
Three days, three nights,
She did not stir:
Three days, three nights,
Were one to her,
Who never closed her eyes
From sunset to sunrise,
From dawn to evenfall:
Her tearless, staring eyes,
That seeing naught, saw all.

The fourth night when I came from work,
I found her at my door.
"And will you cut a stone for him?"
She said: and spoke no more:
But followed me, as I went in,
And sank upon a chair;
And curdled the warm blood in me,
Those eyes that cut me to the bone,
And pierced my marrow like cold steel.

And so I rose, and sought a stone;
And cut it, smooth and square:
And, as I worked, she sat and watched,
Beside me, in her chair.
Night after night, by candlelight,
I cut her lover's name:
Night after night, so still and white,
And like a ghost she came;
And sat beside me in her chair;
And watched with eyes aflame.
She eyed each stroke;
And hardly stirred:
She never spoke
A single word:
And not a sound or murmur broke
The quiet, save the mallet-stroke.
With still eyes ever on my hands,
With eyes that seemed to burn my hands,

My wincing, overwearied hands,
She watched, with bloodless lips apart,
And silent, indrawn breath:
And every stroke my chisel cut,
Death cut still deeper in her heart:
The two of us were chiseling,
Together, I and death.

And when at length the job was done,
And I had laid the mallet by,
As if, at last, her peace were won,
She breathed his name; and, with a sigh,
Passed slowly through the open door:
And never crossed my threshold more.

Next night I labored late, alone.
To cut her name upon the stone.

WILFRID WILSON GIBSON

Requiescat

Tread lightly, she is near
 Under the snow,
Speak gently, she can hear
 The daisies grow.

All her bright golden hair
 Tarnished with rust,
She that was young and fair
 Fallen to dust.

Lily-like, white as snow,
 She hardly knew
She was a woman, so
 Sweetly she grew.

Coffin-board, heavy stone,
 Lie on her breast;
I vex my heart alone,
 She is at rest.

Peace, peace; she cannot hear
 Lyre or sonnet;
All my life's buried here.
 Heap earth upon it.

OSCAR WILDE

BROTHERHOOD

The Human Touch

'Tis the human touch in this world that counts,
    The touch of your hand and mine,
Which means far more to the fainting heart
    Than shelter and bread and wine;
For shelter is gone when the night is o'er,
    And bread lasts only a day,
But the touch of the hand and the sound of the voice
    Sing on in the soul alway.

SPENCER MICHAEL FREE

The House by the Side of the Road

There are hermit souls that live withdrawn
    In the peace of their self-content;
There are souls, like stars, that dwell apart,
    In a fellowless firmament;
There are pioneer souls that blaze their paths
    Where highways never ran;
But let me live by the side of the road
    And be a friend to man.

Let me live in a house by the side of the road,
    Where the race of men go by—
The men who are good and the men who are bad,
    As good and as bad as I.
I would not sit in the scorner's seat,
    Or hurl the cynic's ban;
Let me live in a house by the side of the road
    And be a friend to man.

I see from my house by the side of the road,
　　By the side of the highway of life,
The men who press with the ardor of hope,
　　The men who are faint with the strife.
But I turn not away from their smiles
　　　　nor their tears—
　　Both parts of an infinite plan;
Let me live in my house by the side of the road
　　And be a friend to man.

Let me live in my house by the side of the road
　　Where the race of men go by—
They are good, they are bad, they are weak,
　　　　they are strong,
　　Wise, foolish—so am I.
Then why should I sit in the scorner's seat
　　Or hurl the cynic's bar?—
Let me live in my house by the side of the road
　　And be a friend to man.

SAM WALTER FOSS

Welcome Over the Door of an Old Inn

Hail, Guest! We ask not what thou art;
If Friend, we greet thee, hand and heart;
If Stranger, such no longer be;
If Foe, our love shall conquer thee.

ARTHUR GUITERMAN

What Was His Creed?

What was his creed?
I do not know his creed, I only know
That here below, he walked the common road
And lifted many a load, lightened the task,
Brightened the day for others toiling on a weary way:
This, his only meed; I do not know his creed.

His creed? I care not what his creed;
Enough that never yielded he to greed,
But served a brother in his daily need;
Plucked many a thorn and planted many a flower;
Glorified the service of each hour;
Had faith in God, himself, and fellow-men;—
Perchance he never thought in terms of creed,
I only know he lived a life, in deed!

H.N. FIFER

The Voice of God

I sought to hear the voice of God,
   And climbed the topmost steeple.
But God declared: "Go down again,
   I dwell among the people."

LOUIS I. NEWMAN

Plea for Tolerance

If we but knew what forces helped to mold
    The lives of others from their earliest years—
    Knew something of their background, joys and
        tears,
And whether or not their youth was drear and cold,
Or if some dark belief had taken hold
    And kept them shackled, torn with doubts and
        fears
    So long it crushed the force that perseveres
And made their hearts grow prematurely old,—

Then we might judge with wiser, kindlier sight,
    And learn to put aside our pride and scorn . . .
Perhaps no one can ever quite undo
    His faults or wholly banish some past blight—
The tolerant mind is purified, reborn,
    And lifted upward to a saner view.

MARGARET E. BRUNER

Outwitted

He drew a circle that shut me out—
Heretic, rebel, a thing to flout.
But Love and I had the wit to win:
We drew a circle that took him in!

EDWIN MARKHAM

Who Are My People?

My people? Who are they?
I went into the church where the congregation
Worshipped my God. Were they my people?
I felt no kinship to them as they knelt there.
My people! Where are they?
I went into the land where I was born,
Where men spoke my language. . .
I was a stranger there.
"My people," my soul cried. "Who are my people?"

Last night in the rain I met an old man
Who spoke a language I do not speak,
Which marked him as one who does not
        know my God.
With apologetic smile he offered me
The shelter of his patched umbrella.
I met his eyes . . . And then I knew. . . .

ROSA ZAGNONI MARINONI

CELEBRATION

Ring Out, Wild Bells

Ring out, wild bells, to the wild sky,
   The flying cloud, the frosty light:
   The year is dying in the night;
Ring out, wild bells, and let him die.

Ring out the old, ring in the new,
   Ring, happy bells, across the snow:
   The year is going, let him go;
Ring out the false, ring in the true.

ALFRED, LORD TENNYSON

Trees

I think that I shall never see
A poem lovely as a tree.

A tree whose hungry mouth is prest
Against the earth's sweet flowing breast;

A tree that looks at God all day,
And lifts her leafy arms to pray;

A tree that may in Summer wear
A nest of robins in her hair;

Upon whose bosom snow has lain;
Who intimately lives with rain.

Poems are made by fools like me,
But only God can make a tree.

JOYCE KILMER

The Daffodils

I wandered lonely as a cloud
    That floats on high o'er vales and hills,
When all at once I saw a crowd,
    A host, of golden daffodils,
Beside the lake, beneath the trees,
Fluttering and dancing in the breeze.

Continuous as the stars that shine
    And twinkle on the milky way,
They stretched in never-ending line
    Along the margin of a bay:
Ten thousand saw I at a glance
Tossing their heads in sprightly dance.

The waves beside them danced, but they
    Out-did the sparkling waves in glee:
A Poet could not but be gay
    In such a jocund company!
I gazed—and gazed—but little thought
What wealth the show to me had brought:

For oft, when on my couch I lie
    In vacant or in pensive mood,
They flash upon that inward eye
    Which is the bliss of solitude;
And then my heart with pleasure fills,
And dances with the daffodils.

WILLIAM WORDSWORTH

Holidays

The holiest of all holidays are those
Kept by ourselves in silence and apart;
The secret anniversaries of the heart.

HENRY WADSWORTH LONGFELLOW

A Thing of Beauty

A thing of beauty is a joy for ever:
Its loveliness increases; it will never
Pass into nothingness; but still will keep
A bower quiet for us, and a sleep
Full of sweet dreams, and health, and quiet breathing.
Therefore, on every morrow, are we wreathing
A flowery band to bind us to the earth,
Spite of despondence, of the inhuman dearth
Of noble natures, of the gloomy days,
Of all the unhealthy and o'er-darkened ways
Made for our searching: yes, in spite of all,
Some shape of beauty moves away the pall
From our dark spirits.

JOHN KEATS

Leisure

What is this life if, full of care,
We have no time to stand and stare.

No time to stand beneath the boughs
And stare as long as sheep or cows.

No time to see, when woods we pass,
Where squirrels hide their nuts in grass.

No time to see, in broad daylight,
Streams full of stars, like skies at night.

No time to turn at Beauty's glance,
And watch her feet, how they can dance.

No time to wait till her mouth can
Enrich that smile her eyes began.

A poor life this if, full of care,
We have no time to stand and stare.

WILLIAM HENRY DAVIES

Sea-Fever

I must go down to the seas again, to the lonely sea
    and the sky,
And all I ask is a tall ship and a star to steer her by,
And the wheel's kick and the wind's song and the
    white sail's shaking,
And a gray mist on the sea's face and a gray dawn
    breaking.

I must go down to the seas again, for the call of the
    running tide
Is a wild call and a clear call that may not be denied;
And all I ask is a windy day with the white clouds
    flying,
And the flung spray and the blown spume, and the
    sea-gulls crying.

I must go down to the seas again to the vagrant gypsy
    life.
To the gull's way and the whale's way where the
    wind's like a whetted knife;
And all I ask is a merry yarn from a laughing fellow-
    rover,
And quiet sleep and a sweet dream when the long
    trick's over.

JOHN MASEFIELD

There Is No Death

There is no death! The stars go down
 To rise upon some other shore,
And bright in heaven's jeweled crown
 They shine for evermore.

There is no death! The dust we tread
 Shall change beneath the summer showers
To golden grain or mellow fruit
 Or rainbow-tinted flowers.

There is no death! The leaves may fall,
 The flowers may fade and pass away—
They only wait, through wintry hours,
 The coming of the May.

The bird-like voice, whose joyous tones
 Made glad this scene of sin and strife,
Sings now an everlasting song
 Amid the tree of life.

And ever near us, though unseen,
 The dear immortal spirits tread;
For all the boundless universe
 Is Life—there are no dead!

JOHN LUCKEY MCCREERY

The Village Blacksmith

Under a spreading chestnut tree
   The village smithy stands;
The smith, a mighty man is he,
   With large and sinewy hands;
And the muscles of his brawny arms
   Are strong as iron bands.

His hair is crisp, and black, and long,
   His face is like the tan;
His brow is wet with honest sweat,
   He earns whate'er he can,
And looks the whole world in the face,
   For he owes not any man.

Week in, week out, from morn till night,
   You can hear his bellows blow;
You can hear him swing his heavy sledge,
   With measured beat and slow,
Like a sexton ringing the village bell,
   When the evening sun is low.

And children coming home from school
  Look in at the open door;
They love to see the flaming forge,
  And hear the bellows roar,
And catch the burning sparks that fly
  Like chaff from a threshing floor.

He goes on Sunday to the church,
  And sits among his boys;
He hears the parson pray and preach,
  He hears his daughter's voice,
Singing in the village choir,
  And it makes his heart rejoice.

It sounds to him like her mother's voice,
  Singing in Paradise!
He needs must think of her once more,
  How in the grave she lies;
And with his hard, rough hand he wipes
  A tear out of his eyes.

Toiling,—rejoicing,—sorrowing,
   Onward through life he goes;
Each morning sees some task begin,
   Each evening sees it close;
Something attempted, something done,
   Has earned a night's repose.

Thanks, thanks to thee, my worthy friend,
   For the lesson thou hast taught!
Thus at the flaming forge of life
   Our fortunes must be wrought;
Thus on its sounding anvil shaped
   Each burning deed and thought!

HENRY WADSWORTH LONGFELLOW

Chicago

Hog Butcher for the World,
Tool maker, Stacker of Wheat,
Player with Railroads and the Nation's Freight
   Handler;
Stormy, husky, brawling,
City of the Big Shoulders:

They tell me you are wicked and I believe them,
   for I have seen your painted women under the
   gas lamps luring the farm boys.
 And they tell me you are crooked and I answer:
   Yes, it is true I have seen the gunman kill and
   go free to kill again.
And they tell me you are brutal and my reply is:
   On the faces of women and children I have
   seen the marks of wanton hunger.
And having answered so I turn once more to
   those who sneer at this my city, and I give
   them back the sneer and say to them:
Come and show me another city with lifted head
   singing so proud to be alive and coarse and
   strong and cunning.
Flinging magnetic cures amid the toil of piling
   job on job, here is a tall bold slugger set vivid
   against the little soft cities;

Fierce as a dog with tongue lapping for action,
  cunning as a savage pitted against the
  wilderness,
     Bareheaded,
     Shoveling,
     Wrecking,
     Planning,
     Building, breaking, rebuilding
Under the smoke, dust all over his mouth,
  laughing with white teeth,
Under the terrible burden of destiny laughing as a
  young man laughs,
Laughing even as an ignorant fighter laughs who
  has never lost a battle,
Bragging and laughing that under his wrist is the
  pulse, and under his ribs the heart of the
  people.
               Laughing!
Laughing the stormy, husky, brawling laughter
  of Youth, half-naked, sweating, proud to be
  Hog Butcher, Tool Maker, Stacker of Wheat,
  Player with Railroads and Freight Handler to
  the Nation.

CARL SANDBURG

CHILDREN

Making A Man

Hurry the baby as fast as you can,
Hurry him, worry him, make him a man.
Off with his baby clothes, get him in pants,
Feed him on brain foods and make him advance.
Hustle him, soon as he's able to walk,
Into a grammar school; cram him with talk.
Fill his poor head full of figures and facts,
Keep on a-jamming them in till it cracks.
Once boys grew up at a rational rate,
Now we develop a man while you wait,
Rush him through college, compel him to grab,
Of every known subject a dip and a dab.
Get him in business and after the cash,
All by the time he can grow a mustache
Let him forget he was ever a boy,
Make gold his god and its jingle his joy.
Keep him a-hustling and clear out of breath,
Until he wins—nervous prostration and death.

NIXON WATERMAN

Where Did You Come From?

Where did you come from, Baby dear?
Out of the everywhere into here.

Where did you get your eyes so blue?
Out of the sky as I came through.

What makes the light in them sparkle and spin?
Some of the starry spikes left in.

Where did you get that little tear?
I found it waiting when I got here.

What makes your forehead so smooth and high?
A soft hand stroked it as I went by.

What makes your cheek like a warm white rose?
I saw something better than anyone knows.

Whence that three-corner'd smile of bliss?
Three angels gave me at once a kiss.

Where did you get this pearly ear?
God spoke, and it came out to hear.

Where did you get those arms and hands?
Love made itself into hooks and bands.

Feet, whence did you come, you darling things?
From the same box as the cherubs' wings.

How did they all come just to be you?
God thought of me, and so I grew.

But how did you come to us, you dear?
God thought of you, and so I am here.

GEORGE MACDONALD

On Going Home for Christmas

He little knew the sorrow that was in his vacant
    chair;
He never guessed they'd miss him, or he'd surely have
    been there;
He couldn't see his mother or the lump that filled her
    throat,
Or the tears that started falling as she read his hasty
    note;
And he couldn't see his father, sitting sorrowful and
    dumb,
Or he never would have written that he thought he
    couldn't come.

He little knew the gladness that his presence would
    have made,
And the joy it would have given, or he never would
    have stayed.
He didn't know how hungry had the little mother
    grown
Once again to see her baby and to claim him for her
    own.

He didn't guess the meaning of his visit Christmas
  Day
Or he never would have written that he couldn't get
  away.

He couldn't see the fading of the cheeks that once
  were pink,
And the silver in the tresses; and he didn't stop to
  think
How the years are passing swiftly, and next Christmas
  it might be
There would be no home to visit and no mother dear
  to see.
He didn't think about it—I'll not say he didn't care.
He was heedless and forgetful or he'd surely have
  been there.

Are you going home for Christmas? Have you written
    you'll be there?
Going home to kiss the mother and to show her that
    you care?
Going home to greet the father in a way to make him
    glad?
If you're not I hope there'll never come a time you'll
    wish you had.
Just sit down and write a letter—it will make their
    heartstrings hum
With a tune of perfect gladness—if you'll tell them
    that you'll come.

EDGAR GUEST

On Children

Your children are not your children.
They are the sons and daughters of Life's longing for
      itself.
They come through you but not from you,
And though they are with you yet they belong not to
      you.

You may give them your love but not your thoughts,
For they have their own thoughts.
You may house their bodies but not their souls,
For their souls dwell in the house of tomorrow, which
      you cannot visit, not even in your dreams.
You may strive to be like them, but seek not to make
      them like you.
For life goes not backward nor tarries with yesterday.

KAHLIL GIBRAN

To a New Daughter-in-Law

Forgive me if I speak possessively of him
    Who now is yours, yet still is mine;
Call it the silver cord disparagingly
    And weave new colors in an old design,
Yet know the warp was started long ago
    By faltering steps, by syllable and sound,
By all the years in which I watched him grow. . . .
    By all the seasons' turnings are we bound.

But now, I loose the cord, untie the knot,
    Unravel years so he is yours alone
And if there is a message I forgot
    Or something that could help you had you
        known,
        I shall be waiting, hoping you will see
        That him you love, is also *loved by me*.

AUTHOR UNKNOWN

To My Son

Do you know that your soul is of my soul such part,
That you seem to be fibre and cord of my heart?
None other can pain me as you, dear, can do,
None other can please me or praise me as you.

Remember the world will be quick with its blame
If shadow or stain ever darken your name,
"Like mother like son" is a saying so true,
The world will judge largely of "Mother" by you.

Be yours then the task, if task it shall be
To force the proud world to do homage to me,
Be sure it will say when its verdict you've won,
"She reaped as she sowed, Lo! this is her son."

MARGARET JOHNSTON GRIFFIN

Patty-Poem

She never puts her toys away;
Just leaves them scattered where they lay—
I try to scold her, and I say
   "You make me mad!"

But when to bed she has to chase,
The toys she left about the place
Remind me of her shining face,
   And make me glad.

When she grows up and gathers poise
I'll miss her harum-scarum noise,
And look in vain for scattered toys—
   And I'll be sad.

NICK KENNY

COMPASSION

If I Can Stop One Heart From Breaking

If I can stop one heart from breaking,
    I shall not live in vain;
If I can ease one life the aching,
    Or cool one pain,
Or help one lonely person
    Into happiness again
I shall not live in vain.

EMILY DICKINSON

Prayer for Shut-ins

Because, dear Lord, their way is rough and steep,
And some are sore perplexed, and some do weep,
We come to ask that Thou wilt show the way
And give Thy rod and staff to be their stay.

Especially, dear Lord, for these we ask,
Who have not strength to meet their task;
And for all weary on the road
Please give fresh courage, ease their load.

RUTH WINANT WHEELER

Life Lesson

There! little girl; don't cry!
   They have broken your doll, I know;
      And your tea-set blue,
      And your play-house, too,
   Are things of the long ago;
      But childish troubles will soon pass by
      There! little girl; don't cry!

There! little girl; don't cry!
   They have broken your slate, I know;
      And the glad, wild ways
      Of your school-girl days
   Are things of the long ago;
      But life and love will soon come by.
      There! little girl; don't cry!

There! little girl; don't cry!
   They have broken your heart, I know;
      And the rainbow gleams
      Of your youthful dreams
   Are things of the long ago;
      But heaven holds all for which you sigh.
      There! little girl; don't cry!

JAMES WHITCOMB RILEY

Song of the Shirt

With fingers weary and worn,
    With eyelids heavy and red,
A woman sat in unwomanly rags,
    Plying her needle and thread—
Stitch! stitch! stitch!
    In poverty, hunger, and dirt,
And still with a voice of dolorous pitch
    She sang the "Song of the Shirt!"

"Work—work—work
    Till the brain begins to swim;
Work—work—work
    Till the eyes are heavy and dim!
Seam, and gusset, and band,
    Band, and gusset, and seam,
Till over the buttons I fall asleep,
    And sew them on in a dream!

"O men, with sisters dear!
    O men, with mothers and wives!
It is not linen you're wearing out,
    But human creatures' lives!
Stitch—stitch—stitch!
    In poverty, hunger, and dirt —
Sewing at once, with a double thread,
    A shroud as well as a shirt!

"But why do I talk of Death—
    That phantom of grisly bone?
I hardly fear his terrible shape,
    It seems so like my own,—
It seems so like my own
    Because of the fasts I keep;
O God! that bread should be so dear,
    And flesh and blood so cheap!

"Work! work! work!
    My labor never flags;
And what are its wages? A bed of straw,
    A crust of bread—and rags.
That shattered roof—and this naked floor—
    A table—a broken chair—
And a wall so bland, my shadow I thank
    For sometimes falling there!

"Work—work—work!
    From weary chime to chime!
Work—work—work!
    As prisoners work for crime!
Band, and gusset, and seam,
    Seam, and gusset, and band —
Till the heart is sick and the brain benumbed,
    As well as the weary hand.

"Work—work—work!
    In the dull December light!
And work—work—work!
    When the weather is warm and bright!
While underneath the eaves
    The brooding swallows cling,
As if to show me their sunny backs,
    And twit me with the spring.

"Oh, but for one short hour—
    A respite, however brief!
No blessed leisure for love or hope,
    But only time for grief!
A little weeping would ease my heart;
    But in their briny bed
My tears must stop, for every drop
    Hinders needle and thread!"

With fingers weary and worn,
    With eyelids heavy and red,
A woman sat in unwomanly rags,
    Plying her needle and thread—
Stitch! stitch! stitch!
    In poverty, hunger, and dirt;
And still with a voice of dolorous pitch—
Would that its tone could reach the rich!—
    She sang this "Song of the Shirt."

THOMAS HOOD

Charity

There is so much good in the worst of us,
And so much bad in the best of us,
That it ill behooves any of us
To find fault with the rest of us.

AUTHOR UNKNOWN

Fleurette

My leg? It's off at the knee.
Do I miss it? Well, some. You see
I've had it since I was born;
And lately a devilish corn.
(I rather chuckle with glee
To think how I've fooled that corn.)

But I'll hobble around all right.
It isn't that, it's my face.
Oh I know I'm a hideous sight,
Hardly a thing in place;
Sort of gargoyle, you'd say.
Nurse won't give me a glass,
But I see the folks as they pass
Shudder and turn away;
Turn away in distress. . .
Mirror enough, I guess.

I'm gay! You bet I *am* gay;
But I wasn't a while ago.
If you'd seen me even to-day,
The darndest picture of woe,
With this Caliban mug of mine,
So ravaged and raw and red,
Turned to the wall—in fine,
Wishing that I was dead. . . .

So over the blanket's rim
I raised my terrible face,
And I saw—how I envied him!
A girl of such delicate grace;
Sixteen, all laughter and love;
As gay as a linnet, and yet
As tenderly sweet as a dove;
Half woman, half child—Fleurette.

What has happened since then,
Since I lay with my face to the wall,
The most despairing of men?
Listen! I'll tell you all.

That *poilu* across the way,
With the shrapnel wound in his head,
Has a sister: she came to-day
To sit awhile by his bed.
All morning I heard him fret:
"Oh, when will she come, Fleurette?"

Then sudden, a joyous cry;
The tripping of little feet;
The softest, tenderest sigh;
A voice so fresh and sweet;
Clear as a silver bell,
Fresh as the morning dews:
"C'est toi, c'est toi, Marcel!
Mon frère, comme je suis heureuse!"

Then I turned to the wall again.
(I was awfully blue, you see,)
And I thought with a bitter pain:
"Such visions are not for me."

So there like a log I lay,
All hidden, I thought, from view,
When sudden I heard her say:
"Ah! Who is that *malheureux?*"
Then briefly I heard him tell
(However he came to know)
How I'd smothered a bomb that fell
Into the trench, and so
None of my men were hit,
Though it busted me up a bit.

Well, I didn't quiver an eye,
And he chattered and there she sat;
And I fancied I heard her sigh—
But I wouldn't just swear to that.
And maybe she wasn't so bright,
Though she talked in a merry strain,
And I closed my eyes ever so tight,
Yet I saw her ever so plain:
Her dear little tilted nose,
Her delicate, dimpled chin,
Her mouth like a budding rose,
And the glistening pearls within;
Her eyes like the violet:
Such a rare little queen—Fleurette.

And at last when she rose to go,
The light was a little dim,
And I ventured to peep, and so
I saw her, graceful and slim,
And she kissed him and kissed him, and oh
How I envied and envied him!

So when she was gone I said
In rather a dreary voice
To him of the opposite bed:
"Ah, friend, how you must rejoice!
But me, I'm a thing of dread.
For me nevermore the bliss,
The thrill of a woman's kiss."

Then I stopped, for lo! she was there,
And a great light shone in her eyes.
And me! I could only stare,
I was taken so by surprise,
When gently she bent her head:
"May I kiss you, Sergeant?" she said.

Then she kissed my burning lips
With her mouth like a scented flower,
And I thrilled to the finger-tips,
And I hadn't even the power
To say: "God bless you, dear!"
And I felt such a precious tear
Fall on my withered cheek,
And darn it! I couldn't speak.
And so she went sadly away,
And I knew that my eyes were wet.
Ah, not to my dying day
Will I forget, forget!
Can you wonder now I am gay?
God bless her, that little Fleurette!

ROBERT SERVICE

The Rime of the
Ancient Mariner

PART I

It is an ancient Mariner,
    And he stoppeth one of three.
'By thy long grey beard and glittering eye,
    Now wherefore stopp'st thou me?

The Bridegroom's doors are opened wide,
    And I am next of kin;
The guests are met, the feast is set:
    May'st hear the merry din.'

He holds him with his skinny hand,
    'There was a ship,' quoth he.
'Hold off! unhand me, grey-beard loon!"
    Eftsoons his hand dropt he.

He holds him with his glittering eye—
    The Wedding-Guest stood still,
And listens like a three years' child:
    The Mariner hath his will.

The Wedding-Guest sat on a stone:
  He cannot choose but hear;
And thus spake on that ancient man,
  The bright-eyed Mariner.

'The ship was cheered, the harbour cleared,
  Merrily did we drop
Below the kirk, below the hill,
  Below the lighthouse top.

The Sun came up upon the left,
  Out of the sea came he!
And he shone bright, and on the right
  Went down into the sea.

Higher and higher every day,
  Till over the mast at noon—
The Wedding-Guest here beat his breast,
  For he heard the loud bassoon.

The bride hath paced into the hall,
  Red as a rose is she;
Nodding their heads before her goes
  The merry minstrelsy.

The Wedding-Guest he beat his breast,
　　Yet he cannot choose but hear;
And thus spake on that ancient man,
　　The bright-eyed Mariner.

'And now the Storm-blast came, and he
　　Was tyrannous and strong:
He struck with his o'ertaking wings,
　　And chased us south along.

With sloping masts and dipping prow,
　　As who pursued with yell and blow
Still treads the shadow of his foe,
　　And forward bends his head,
The ship drove fast, loud roared the blast,
　　And southward aye we fled.

And now there came both mist and snow,
　　And it grew wondrous cold:
And ice, mast-high, came floating by,
　　As green as emerald.

And through the drifts the snowy clifts
　　Did send a dismal sheen:
Nor shapes of men nor beasts we ken—
　　The ice was all between.

The ice was here, the ice was there,
    The ice was all around:
It cracked and growled, and roared and howled,
    Like noises in a swound!

At length did cross an Albatross,
    Thorough the fog it came;
As if it had been a Christian soul,
    We hailed it in God's name.

It ate the food it ne'er had eat,
    And round and round it flew.
The ice did split with a thunder-fit;
    The helmsman steer'd us through!

And a good south wind sprung up behind;
    The Albatross did follow,
And every day, for food or play,
    Came to the mariners' hollo!

In mist or cloud, on mast or shroud,
    It perched for vespers nine;
Whiles all the night, through fog-smoke white,
    Glimmered the whole moonshine.'

'God save thee, ancient Mariner,
    From the fiends, that plague thee thus!—
Why look'st thou so?'—'With my crossbow
    I shot the Albatross.

PART II

'The Sun now rose upon the right:
    Out of the sea came he,
Still hid in mist, and on the left
    Went down into the sea.

And the good south wind still blew behind,
    But no sweet bird did follow,
Nor any day for food or play
    Came to the mariners' hollo!

And I had done a hellish thing,
    And it would work 'em woe:
For all averred I had killed the bird
    That made the breeze to blow.
Ah wretch! said they, the bird to slay,
    That made the breeze to blow!

Nor dim nor red, like God's own head,
  The glorious Sun uprist:
Then all averred I had killed the bird
  That brought the fog and mist.
'Twas right, said they, such birds to slay
  That bring the fog and mist.

The fair breeze blew, the white foam flew,
  The furrow followed free;
We were the first that ever burst
  Into that silent sea.

Down dropt the breeze, the sails dropt down,
  'Twas sad as sad could be;
And we did speak only to break
  The silence of the sea!

All in a hot and copper sky,
  The bloody Sun, at noon,
Right up above the mast did stand,
  No bigger than the Moon.

Day after day, day after day,
  We stuck, nor breath nor motion;
As idle as a painted ship
  Upon a painted ocean.

Water, water, everywhere,
   And all the boards did shrink;
Water, water everywhere
   Nor any drop to drink.

The very deep did rot: O Christ!
   That ever this should be!
Yea, slimy things did crawl with legs
   Upon the slimy sea.

About, about, in reel and rout
   The death-fires danced at night;
The water, like a witch's oils,
   Burnt green, and blue, and white.

And some in dreams assured were
   Of the Spirit that plagued us so;
Nine fathom deep he had followed us
   From the land of mist and snow.

And every tongue, through utter drought,
   Was withered at the root;
We could not speak, no more than if
   We had been choked with soot.

Ah! well a-day! what evil looks
Had I from old and young!
Instead of the cross, the Albatross
About my neck was hung.

PART III

'There passed a weary time. Each throat
Was parched, and glazed each eye.
A weary time! a weary time!
How glazed each weary eye!
When, looking westward, I beheld
A something in the sky.

At first it seemed a little speck,
And then it seemed a mist;
It moved and moved, and took at last
A certain shape, I wist.

A speck, a mist, a shape, I wist!
And still it neared and neared:
As if it dodged a water-sprite,
It plunged, and tacked and veered.

With throats unslaked, with black lips baked,
We could nor laugh nor wail;
Through utter drought all dumb we stood!
I bit my arm, I sucked the blood.
And cried, A sail! a sail!

With throats unslaked, with black lips baked,
    Agape they heard me call:
Gramercy! they for joy did grin,
    And all at once their breath drew in,
As they were drinking all.

See! see! (I cried) she tacks no more!
    Hither to work us weal—
Without a breeze, without a tide,
    She steadies with upright keel!

The western wave was all aflame,
    The day was well nigh done!
Almost upon the western wave
    Rested the broad, bright Sun;
When that strange shape drove suddenly
    Betwixt us and the Sun.

And straight the Sun was flecked with bars
    (Heaven's Mother send us grace!),
As if through a dungeon-grate he peered
    With broad and burning face.

Alas! (thought I, and my heart beat loud)
    How fast she nears and nears!
Are those *her* sails that glance in the Sun,
    Like restless gossameres?

Are those *her* ribs through which the Sun
　　Did peer, as through a grate?
And is that Woman all her crew?
　　Is that a Death? and are there two?
Is Death that Woman's mate?

Her lips were red, her looks were free,
　　Her locks were yellow as gold:
Her skin was as white as leprosy,
　　The Nightmare Life-in-Death was she,
Who thicks man's blood with cold.

The naked hulk alongside came,
　　And the twain were casting dice;
"The game is done! I've won! I've won!"
　　Quoth she, and whistles thrice.

The Sun's rim dips; the stars rush out:
　　At one stride comes the dark;
With far-heard whisper, o'er the sea,
　　Off shot the spectre-bark.

We listened and looked sideways up!
　　Fear at my heart, as at a cup,
My life-blood seemed to sip!
　　The stars were dim, and thick the night,
The steerman's face by his lamp gleamed white;
　　From the sails the dew did drip—

Till clomb above the eastern bar
    The horned Moon, with one bright star
Within the nether tip.

One after one, by the star-dogged Moon,
    Too quick for groan or sigh,
Each turned his face with a ghastly pang,
    And cursed me with his eye.

Four times fifty living men
    (And I heard nor sigh nor groan),
With heavy thump, a lifeless lump,
    They dropped down one by one.

The souls did from their bodies fly—
    They fled to bliss or woe!
And every soul, it passed me by
    Like the whizz of my cross-bow!'

PART IV

'I fear thee, ancient Mariner!
    I fear thy skinny hand!
And thou art long, and lank, and brown,
    As is the ribbed sea-sand.

I fear thee and thy glittering eye,
  And thy skinny hand so brown.'—
'Fear not, fear not, thou Wedding Guest!
  This body dropt not down.

Alone, alone, all, all alone
  Alone on a wide, wide sea!
And never a saint took pity on
  My soul in agony.

The many men, so beautiful!
  And they all dead did lie:
And a thousand thousand slimy things
  Lived on; and so did I.

I looked upon the rotting sea,
  And drew my eyes away;
I looked upon the rotting deck,
  And there the dead men lay.

I looked to heaven, and tried to pray;
  But or ever a prayer had gusht,
A wicked whisper came, and made
  My heart as dry as dust.

I closed my lids, and kept them close,
   And the balls like pulses beat;
But the sky and the sea, and the sea and the sky,
   Lay like a load on my weary eye,
And the dead were at my feet.

The cold sweat melted from their limbs,
   Nor rot nor reek did they:
The look with which they looked on me
   Had never passed away.

An orphan's curse would drag to hell
   A spirit from on high;
But oh! more horrible than that
   Is the curse in a dead man's eye!
Seven days, seven nights, I saw that curse,
   And yet I could not die.

The moving Moon went up the sky,
   And nowhere did abide;
Softly she was going up,
   And a star or two beside—

Her beams bemocked the sultry main,
　Like April hoar-frost spread;
But where the ship's huge shadow lay,
　The charmed water burnt alway
A still and awful red.

Beyond the shadow of the ship,
　I watched the water-snakes:
They moved in tracks of shining white,
　And when they reared, the elfish light
Fell off in hoary flakes.

Within the shadow of the ship
　I watched their rich attire:
Blue, glossy green, and velvet black,
　They coiled and swam; and every track
Was a flash of golden fire.

O happy living things! no tongue
　Their beauty might declare:
A spring of love gushed from my heart,
　And I blessed them unaware:
Sure my kind saint took pity on me,
　And I blessed them unaware.

The selfsame moment I could pray;
    And from my neck so free
The Albatross fell off, and sank
    Like lead into the sea.

PART V

'O sleep! it is a gentle thing,
    Beloved from pole to pole!
To Mary Queen the praise be given!
    She sent the gentle sleep from Heaven,
That slid into my soul.

The silly buckets on the deck,
    That had so long remained,
I dreamt that they were filled with dew;
    And when I awoke, it rained.

My lips were wet, my throat was cold.
    My garments all were dank;
Sure I had drunken in my dreams,
    And still my body drank.

I moved, and could not feel my limbs:
   I was so light—almost
I thought that I had died in sleep,
   And was a blessed ghost.

And soon I heard a roaring wind:
   It did not come anear;
But with its sound it shook the sails,
   That were so thin and sere.

The upper air burst into life;
   And a hundred fire-flags sheen;
To and fro they were hurried about!
   And to and fro, and in and out,
The wan stars danced between.

And the coming wind did roar more loud,
   And the sails did sigh like sedge;
And the rain poured down from one black cloud;
   The Moon was at its edge.

The thick black cloud was cleft, and still
   The Moon was at its side;
Like waters shot from some high crag,
   The lightning fell with never a jag,
A river steep and wide.

The loud wind never reached the ship,
  Yet now the ship moved on!
Beneath the lightning and the Moon
  The dead men gave a groan.

They groaned, they stirred, they all uprose,
  Nor spake, nor moved their eyes;
It had been strange, even in a dream,
  To have seen those dead men rise.

The helmsman steered, the ship moved on;
  Yet never a breeze up-blew;
The mariners all 'gan work the ropes,
  Where they were wont to do;
They raised their limbs like lifeless tools—
  We were a ghastly crew.

The body of my brother's son
  Stood by me, knee to knee:
The body and I pulled at one rope,
  But he said naught to me.'

'I fear thee, ancient Mariner!'
  'Be calm, thou Wedding-Guest!
'Twas not those souls that fled in pain,
  Which to their corses came again,
But a troop of spirits blest:

For when it dawned—they dropped their arms,
   And clustered round the mast;
Sweet sounds rose slowly through their mouths,
   And from their bodies passed.

Around, around, flew each sweet sound,
   Then darted to the Sun;
Slowly the sounds came back again,
   Now mixed, now one by one.

Sometimes a-dropping from the sky
   I heard the skylark sing;
Sometimes all little birds that are,
   How they seemed to fill the sea and air
With their sweet jargoning!

And now 'twas like all instruments,
   Now like a lonely flute;
And now it is an angel's song,
   That makes the Heavens be mute.

It ceased; yet still the sails made on
   A pleasant noise till noon,
A noise like of a hidden brook
   In the leafy month of June,
That to the sleeping woods all night
   Singeth a quiet tune.

Till noon we quietly sailed on,
 Yet never a breeze did breathe:
Slowly and smoothly went the ship,
 Moved onward from beneath.

Under the keel nine fathom deep,
 From the land of mist and snow,
The Spirit slid: and it was he
 That made the ship to go.
The sails at noon left off their tune,
 And the ship stood still also.

The Sun, right up above the mast,
 Had fixed her to the ocean:
But in a minute she 'gan stir,
 With a short uneasy motion—
Backwards and forwards half her length
 With a short uneasy motion.

Then like a pawing horse let go,
 She made a sudden bound:
It flung the blood into my head,
 And I fell down in a swound.

How long in that same fit I lay,
    I have not to declare;
But ere my living life returned,
    I heard, and in my soul discerned
Two voices in the air.

"Is it he?" quoth one, "is this the man?
    By Him who died on cross,
With his cruel bow he laid full low
    The harmless Albatross.

The Spirit who bideth by himself
    In the land of mist and snow,
He loved the bird that loved the man
    Who shot him with his bow."

The other was a softer voice,
    As soft as honey-dew:
Quoth he, "The man hath penance done,
    And penance more will do."

PART VI

First Voice:
'"But tell me, tell me! speak again,
    Thy soft response renewing—
What makes that ship drive on so fast?
    What is the Ocean doing?"

Second Voice:

"Still as a slave before his lord,
    The Ocean hath no blast;
His great bright eye most silently
    Up to the Moon is cast—

If he may know which way to go;
    For she guides him smooth or grim.
See, brother, see! how graciously
    She looketh down on him."

First Voice:

"But why drives on that ship so fast,
    Without or wave or wind?"

Second Voice:

"The air is cut away before,
    And closes from behind.

Fly, brother, fly! more high, more high!
    Or we shall be belated:
For slow and slow that ship will go,
    When the Mariner's trance is abated."

I woke, and we were sailing on
  As in a gentle weather:
'Twas night, calm night, the Moon was high;
  The dead men stood together.

All stood together on the deck,
  For a charnel-dungeon fitter:
All fixed on me their stony eyes,
  That in the Moon did glitter.

The pang, the curse, with which they died,
  Had never passed away:
I could not draw my eyes from theirs,
  Nor turn them up to pray.

And now this spell was snapt: once more
  I viewed the ocean green,
And looked far forth, yet little saw
  Of what had else been seen—

Like one that on a lonesome road
  Doth walk in fear and dread,
And having once turned round, walks on,
  And turns no more his head;
Because he knows a frightful fiend
  Doth close behind him tread.

But soon there breathed a wind on me
  Nor sound nor motion made:
Its path was not upon the sea,
  In ripple or in shade.

It raised my hair, it fanned my cheek
  Like a meadow-gale of spring—
It mingled strangely with my fears,
  Yet it felt like a welcoming.

Swiftly, swiftly flew the ship,
  Yet she sailed softly too:
Sweetly, sweetly blew the breeze—
  On me alone it blew.

O dream of joy! is this indeed
  The lighthouse top I see?
Is this the hill? is this the kirk?
  Is this mine own countree?

We drifted o'er the harbour-bar,
  And I with sobs did pray—
O let me be awake, my God!
  Or let me sleep alway.

The harbour-bay was clear as glass,
   So smoothly it was strewn!
And on the bay the moonlight lay,
   And the shadow of the Moon.

The rock shone bright, the kirk no less
   That stands above the rock:
The moonlight steeped in silentness
   The steady weathercock.

And the bay was white with silent light
   Till rising from the same,
Full many shapes, that shadows were,
   In crimson colours came.

A little distance from the prow
   Those crimson shadows were:
I turned my eyes upon the deck—
   O Christ! what saw I there!

Each corse lay flat, lifeless and flat,
   And, by the holy rood!
A man all light, a seraph-man,
   On every corse there stood.

This seraph-band, each waved his hand:
    It was a heavenly sight!
They stood as signals to the land,
    Each one a lovely light.

This seraph-band, each waved his hand,
    No 'voice did they impart—
No voice; but O, the silence sank
    Like music on my heart.

But soon I heard the dash of oars,
    I heard the Pilot's cheer;
My head was turned perforce away,
    And I saw a boat appear.

The Pilot and the Pilot's boy,
    I heard them coming fast:
Dear Lord in Heaven! it was a joy
    The dead men could not blast.

I saw a third—I heard his voice:
    It is the Hermit good!
He singeth loud his godly hymns
    That he makes in the wood.
He'll shrieve my soul, he'll wash away
    The Albatross's blood.

PART VII

'This hermit good lives in that wood
  Which slopes down to the sea.
How loudly his sweet voice he rears!
  He loves to talk with marineres
That come from a far countree.

He kneels at morn, and noon, and eve—
  He hath a cushion plump.
It is the moss that wholly hides
  The rotted old oak-stump.

The skiff-boat neared: I heard them talk,
  "Why, this is strange, I trow!
Where are those lights so many and fair,
  That signal made but now?"

"Strange, by my faith!" the Hermit said—
  "And they answered not our cheer!
The planks look warped! and see those sails
  How thin they are and sere!
I never saw aught like to them,
  Unless perchance it were

Brown skeletons of leaves that lag
   My forest-brook along;
When the ivy-tod is heavy with snow,
   And the owlet whoops to the wolf below,
That eats the she-wolf's young."

"Dear Lord! it hath a fiendish look—
   (The Pilot made reply)
I am a-feared."—"Push on, push on!"
   Said the Hermit cheerily.

The boat came closer to the ship,
   But I nor spake nor stirred;
The boat came close beneath the ship,
   And straight a sound was heard.

Under the water it rumbled on
   Still louder and more dread:
It reached the ship, it split the bay;
   The ship went down like lead.

Stunned by that loud and dreadful sound,
   Which sky and ocean smote,
Like one that hath been seven days drowned
   My body lay afloat;
But swift as dreams, myself I found
   Within the Pilot's boat.

Upon the whirl, where sank the ship,
  The boat spun round and round;
And all was still, save that the hill
  Was telling of the sound.

I moved my lips—the Pilot shriek'd
  And fell down in a fit;
The holy Hermit raised his eyes,
  And prayed where he did sit.

I took the oars: the Pilot's boy,
  Who now doth crazy go,
Laughed loud and long, and all the while
  His eyes went to and fro.
"Ha! ha!" quoth he, "full plain I see
  The Devil knows how to row."

And now, all in my own countree,
  I stood on the firm land!
The Hermit stepped forth from the boat,
  And scarcely he could stand.

"O shrieve me, shrieve me, holy man!"
    The Hermit crossed his brow.
"Say quick," quoth he, "I bid thee say—
    What manner of man art thou?"

Forthwith this frame of mine was wrenched
    With a woful agony
Which forced me to begin my tale;
    And then it left me free.

Since then, at an uncertain hour,
    That agony returns:
And till my ghastly tale is told,
    This heart within me burns.

I pass, like night, from land to land;
    I have strange power of speech;
That moment that his face I see,
    I know the man that must hear me:
To him my tale I teach.

What loud uproar bursts from that door!
 The wedding-guests are there:
But in the garden-bower the bride
 And bride-maids singing are:
And hark, the little vesper bell,
 Which biddeth me to prayer!

O Wedding-Guest! this soul hath been
 Alone on a wide, wide sea:
So lonely 'twas, that God Himself
 Scarce seemed there to be.

O sweeter than the marriage-feast,
 'Tis sweeter far to me,
To walk together to the kirk
 With a goodly company!—

To walk together to the kirk,
 And all together pray
While each to his great Father bends,
 Old men, and babes, and loving friends,
And youths and maidens gay!

Farewell, farewell! but this I tell
  To thee, thou Wedding-Guest!
He prayeth well, who loveth well
  Both man and bird and beast.

He prayeth best, who loveth best
  All things both great and small;
For the dear God who loveth us,
  He made and loveth all.'

The Mariner, whose eye is bright,
  Whose beard with age is hoar,
Is gone: and now the Wedding-Guest
  Turned from the bridegroom's door.

He went like one that hath been stunn'd,
  And is of sense forlorn:
A sadder and a wiser man
  He rose the morrow morn.

SAMUEL TAYLOR COLERIDGE

COURAGE

It Can be Done

The man who misses all the fun
Is he who says, "It can't be done."
In solemn pride he stands aloof
And greets each venture with reproof.
Had he the power he'd efface
The history of the human race;
We'd have no radio or motor cars,
No streets lit by electric stars;
No telegraph nor telephone,
We'd linger in the age of stone.
The world would sleep if things were run
By men who say, "It can't be done."

AUTHOR UNKNOWN

Invictus

Out of the night that covers me,
    Black as the Pit from pole to pole,
I thank whatever gods may be
    For my unconquerable soul.

In the fell clutch of circumstance
    I have not winced nor cried aloud.
Under the bludgeonings of chance
    My head is bloody, but unbowed.

Beyond this place of wrath and tears
    Looms but the horror of the shade,
And yet the menace of the years
    Finds, and shall find me, unafraid.

It matters not how strait the gate,
    How charged with punishments the scroll,
I am the master of my fate:
    I am the captain of my soul.

WILLIAM ERNEST HENLEY

Defeat

No one is beat till he quits,
   No one is through till he stops,
No matter how hard Failure hits,
   No matter how often he drops,
A fellow's not down till he lies
In the dust and refuses to rise.

Fate can slam him and bang him around,
   And batter his frame till he's sore,
But she never can say that he's downed
   While he bobs up serenely for more.
A fellow's not dead till he dies,
Nor beat till no longer he tries.

EDGAR GUEST

You Mustn't Quit

When things go wrong, as they sometimes will,
When the road you're trudging seems all uphill,
When the funds are low and the debts are high
And you want to smile, but you have to sigh,
When care is pressing you down a bit,
Rest! if you must—but never quit.

Life is queer, with its twists and turns,
As every one of us sometimes learns,
And many a failure turns about
When he might have won if he'd stuck it out;
Stick to your task, though the pace seems slow—
You may succeed with one more blow.

Success is failure turned inside out—
The silver tint of the clouds of doubt—
And you never can tell how close you are,
It may be near when it seems afar;
So stick to the fight when you're hardest hit—
It's when things seem worst that YOU MUSTN'T QUIT.

AUTHOR UNKNOWN

If—

If you can keep your head when all about you
    Are losing theirs and blaming it on you;
If you can trust yourself when all men doubt you,
    But make allowance for their doubting too;
If you can wait and not be tired by waiting,
    Or, being lied about, don't deal in lies,
Or, being hated, don't give way to hating,
    And yet don't look too good, nor talk too wise;

If you can dream—and not make dreams your
      master;
    If you can think—and not make thoughts your
      aim;
If you can meet with triumph and disaster
    And treat those two impostors just the same;
If you can bear to hear the truth you've spoken
    Twisted by knaves to make a trap for fools,
Or watch the things you gave your life to broken,
    And stoop and build 'em up with worn out tools;

If you can make one heap of all your winnings
   And risk it on one turn of pitch-and-toss,
And lose, and start again at your beginnings
   And never breathe a word about your loss;
If you can force your heart and nerve and sinew
   To serve your turn long after they are gone,
And so hold on when there is nothing in you
   Except the Will which says to them: "Hold on!"

If you can talk with crowds and keep your virtue,
   Or walk with kings—nor lose the common touch;
If neither foes nor loving friends can hurt you;
   If all men count with you, but none too much;
If you can fill the unforgiving minute
   With sixty seconds' worth of distance run—
Yours is the Earth and everything that's in it,
   And—which is more—you'll be a Man, my son!

RUDYARD KIPLING

Curfew Must Not Ring Tonight

Slowly England's sun was setting o'er the hilltops far
away,
Filling all the land with beauty at the close of one sad
day;
And the last rays kissed the forehead of a man and a
maiden fair,
He with footsteps slow and weary, she with sunny
floating hair;
He with bowed head, sad and thoughtful, she with
lips all cold and white,
Struggling to keep back the murmur, "Curfew must
not ring tonight!"

"Sexton," Bessie's white lips faltered, pointing to the
      prison old,
With its turrets tall and gloomy, with its walls, dark,
      damp and cold—
"I've a lover in the prison, doomed this very night to
      die
At the ringing of the curfew, and no earthly help is
      nigh!
Cromwell will not come till sunset"; and her face
      grew strangely white
As she breathed the husky whisper, "Curfew must not
      ring tonight!"

"Bessie," calmly spoke the sexton—and his accents
      pierced her heart
Like the piercing of an arrow, like a deadly poisoned
      dart—
"Long, long years I've rung the curfew from that
      gloomy, shadowed tower;
Every evening, just at sunset, it has told the twilight
      hour;
I have done my duty ever, tried to do it just and
      right—
Now I'm old I still must do it: Curfew, girl, must ring
      tonight!"

Wild her eyes and pale her features, stern and white
  her thoughtful brow,
And within her secret bosom Bessie made a solemn
  vow.
She had listened while the judges read, without a tear
  or sigh,
"At the ringing of the curfew, Basil Underwood must
  die."
And her breath came fast and faster, and her eyes grew
  large and bright,
As in undertone she murmured, "Curfew must not
  ring tonight!"

With quick step she bounded forward, sprang within
  the old church door,
Left the old man threading slowly paths he'd often
  trod before;
Not one moment paused the maiden, but with eye and
  cheek aglow
Mounted up the gloomy tower, where the bell swung
  to and fro
As she climbed the dusty ladder, on which fell no ray
  of light,
Up and up, her white lips saying, "Curfew shall not
  ring tonight!"

She has reached the topmost ladder, o'er her hangs
      the great dark bell:
Awful is the gloom beneath her, like the pathway
      down to hell!
Lo, the ponderous tongue is swinging.
      'Tis the hour of curfew now,
And the sight has chilled her bosom, stopped her
      breath and paled her brow;
Shall she let it ring? No, never! Flash her eyes with
      sudden light,
And she springs and grasps it firmly:
      "Curfew shall not ring tonight!"

Out she swung, far out; the city seemed a speck of
      light below;
She 'twixt heaven and earth suspended as the bell
      swung to and fro;
And the sexton at the bell rope, old and deaf, heard
      not the bell,
But he thought it still was ringing fair young Basil's
      funeral knell.
Still the maiden clung more firmly, and, with trem-
      bling lips and white,
Said, to hush her heart's wild beating, "Curfew shall
      not ring tonight!"

It was o'er; the bell ceased swaying, and the maiden
      stepped once more
Firmly on the dark old ladder, where for hundred
      years before
Human foot had not been planted; but the brave deed
      she had done
Should be told long ages after—often as the setting
      sun
Should illume the sky with beauty, aged sires, with
      heads of white,
Long should tell the little children, "Curfew did not
      ring that night."

O'er the distant hills came Cromwell; Bessie sees him,
      and her brow,
Full of hope and full of gladness, has no anxious
      traces now.
At his feet she tells her story, shows her hands all
      bruised and torn;
And her face so sweet and pleading, yet with sorrow
      pale and worn,
Touched his heart with sudden pity—lit his eye with
      misty light;
"Go, your lover lives!" said Cromwell; "Curfew shall
      not ring tonight!"

Wide they flung the massive portals, led the prisoner
     forth to die,
All his bright young life before him. 'Neath the
     darkening English sky
Bessie came with flying footsteps, eyes aglow with
     love-light sweet;
Kneeling on the turf beside him, laid a pardon at his
     feet.
In his brave, strong arms he clasped her, kissed the
     face upturned and white,
Whispered, "Darling, you have saved me; curfew will
     not ring tonight."

ROSE HARTWICK THORPE

The Hell-Gate of Soissons

My name is Darino, the poet. You have heard? *Oui,*
Comédie Française.
Perchance it has happened, *mon ami*, you know of
my unworthy lays.
Ah, then you must guess how my fingers are itching
to talk to a pen;
For I was at Soissons, and saw it, the death of the
twelve Englishmen.

My leg, *malheureusement*, I left it behind on the
banks of the Aisne.
Regret? I would pay with the other to witness their
valor again.
A trifle, indeed, I assure you, to give for the honor to
tell
How that handful of British, undaunted, went into the
Gateway of Hell.

Let me draw you a plan of the battle. Here we French
and your Engineers stood;
Over there a detachment of German sharpshooters lay
hid in a wood.
A *mitrailleuse* battery planted on top of this well-
chosen ridge
Held the road for the Prussians and covered the direct
approach to the bridge.

It was madness to dare the dense murder that spewed
      from those ghastly machines.
(Only those who have danced to its music can know
      what the *mitrailleuse* means.)
But the bridge on the Aisne was a menace; our safety
      demanded its fall:
"Engineers—volunteers!" In a body, the Royals stood
      out at the call.

Death at best was the fate of that mission—to their
      glory not one was dismayed.
A party was chosen—and seven survived till the
      powder was laid.
And *they* died with their fuses unlighted. Another
      detachment! Again
A sortie is made—all too vainly. The bridge still
      commanded the Aisne.

We were fighting two foes—Time and Prussia—the
      moments were worth more than troops.
We *must* blow up the bridge. A lone soldier darts out
      from the Royals and swoops
For the fuse! Fate seems with us. We cheer him; he
      answers—our hopes are reborn!
A ball rips his visor—his khaki shows red where
      another has torn.

Will he live—will he last—will he make it? *Hélas!*
    And so near to the goal!
A second, he dies! Then a third one! A fourth! Still the
    Germans take toll!
A fifth, *magnifique!* It is magic! How does he escape
    them? He may. . .
Yes, he *does!* See, the match flares! A rifle rings out
    from the wood and says "Nay!"

Six, seven, eight, nine take their places; six, seven,
    eight, nine brave their hail:
Six, seven, eight, nine—how we count them! But the
    sixth, seventh, eighth, and ninth fail!
A tenth! *Sacré nom!* But these English are soldiers—
    they know how to try;
(He fumbles the place where his jaw was)—they
    show, too, how heroes can die.

Ten we count—ten who ventured unquailing—ten
    there were—and ten are no more!
Yet another salutes and superbly essays where the ten
    failed before.
God of Battles, look down and protect him! Lord, his
    heart is as Thine—let him live!
But the *mitrailleuse* splutters and stutters, and riddles
    him into a sieve.

Then I thought of my sins, and sat waiting the charge
  that we could not withstand.
And I thought of my beautiful Paris, and gave a
  last look at the land,
At France, my *belle France*, in her glory of blue sky
  and green field and wood.
Death with honor, but never surrender. And to die
  with such men—it was good.

They are forming—the bugles are blaring—they will
  cross in a moment and then—
When out of the line of the Royals (your island, *mon
  ami*, breeds men)
Bursts a private, a tawny-haired giant—it was
  hopeless, but *ciel* how he ran!
Bon Dieu please remember the pattern, and make
  many more on his plan!

No cheers from our ranks, and the Germans, they
  halted in wonderment, too;
See, he reaches the bridge; ah! he lights it! I am
  dreaming, it *cannot* be true.
Screams of rage! *Fusillade!* They have killed him! Too
  late though, the good work is done.
By the valor of twelve English martyrs, the Hell-Gate
  of Soissons is won!

HERBERT KAUFMAN

Horatius

Lars Porsena of Clusium
  By the Nine Gods he swore
That the great house of Tarquin
  Should suffer wrong no more.
By the Nine Gods he swore it,
  And named a trysting day,
And bade his messengers ride forth,
East and west and south and north,
  To summon his array.

East and west and south and north
  The messengers ride fast,
And tower and town and cottage
  Have heard the trumpet's blast.
Shame on the false Etruscan
  Who lingers in his home
When Porsena of Clusium
  Is on the march for Rome.

And now hath every city
  Sent up her tale of men;
The foot are fourscore thousand,
  The horse are thousands ten.
Before the gates of Sutirum
  Is met the great array.
A proud man was Lars Porsena
  Upon the trysting day.

Now from the rock Tarpeian,
     Could the wan burghers spy
The line of blazing villages
     Red in the midnight sky.
The fathers of the City,
     They sat all night and day,
For every hour some horseman came
     With tidings of dismay.

I wis, in all the Senate,
     There was no heart so bold,
But sore it ached, and fast it beat,
     When that ill news was told.
Forthwith up rose the Consul,
     Up rose the Fathers all;
In haste they girded up their gowns,
     And hied them to the wall.

They held a council standing
     Before the River-gate;
Short time was there, ye well may guess,
     For musing or debate.
Out spake the Consul roundly:
     "The bridge must straight go down;
For, since Janiculum is lost,
     Naught else can save the town."

Just then a scout came flying,
    All wild with haste and fear:
"To arms! to arms! Sir Consul;
    Lars Porsena is here."
On the low hills to westward
    The Consul fixed his eye,
And saw the swarthy storm of dust
    Rise fast along the sky.

And the Consul's brow was sad,
    And the Consul's speech was low,
And darkly looked he at the wall,
    And darkly at the foe.
"Their van will be upon us
    Before the bridge goes down;
And if they once may win the bridge,
    What hope to save the town?"

Then out spake brave Horatius,
    The Captain of the gate:
"To every man upon this earth
    Death cometh soon or late.
And how can man die better
    Than facing fearful odds,
For the ashes of his fathers
    And the temples of his Gods!

"Hew down the bridge, Sir Consul,
　　With all the speed ye may;
I, with two more to help me,
　　Will hold the foe in play.
In yon strait path a thousand
　　May well be stopped by three.
Now who will stand on either hand,
　　And keep the bridge with me?"

Then out spake Spurius Lartius;
　　A Ramnian proud was he:
"Lo, I will stand at thy right hand,
　　And keep the bridge with thee."
And out spake strong Herminius;
　　Of Titan blood was he:
"I will abide on thy left side,
　　And keep the bridge with thee."

Now while the Three were tightening
　　Their harness on their backs,
The Consul was the foremost man
　　To take in hand an axe:
And Fathers mixed with Commons
　　Seized hatchet, bar, and crow,
And smote upon the planks above,
　　And loosed the props below.

The Three stood calm and silent
    And looked upon the foes,
And a great shout of laughter
    From all the vanguard rose:
And forth three chiefs came spurring
    Before that deep array;
To earth they sprang, their swords they drew,
And lifted high their shields, and flew
    To win the narrow way;

Aunus from green Tifernum,
    Lord of the Hill of Vines;
And Seius, whose eight hundred slaves
    Sicken in Ilva's mines;
And Picus, long to Clusium
    Vassal in peace and war,
Who led to fight his Umbrian powers
From that gray crag where, girt with towers,
The fortress of Nequinum lowers
    O'er the pale waves of Nar.

Stout Lartius hurled down Aunus
    Into the stream beneath:
Herminius struck at Seius,
    And clove him to the teeth:

At Picus brave Horatius
　　Darted one fiery thrust;
And the proud Umbrian's gilded arms
　　Clashed in the bloody dust.

Then Ocnus of Falerii
　　Rushed on the Roman Three;
And Lausulus of Urgo,
　　The rover of the sea;
And Aruns of Volsinium,
　　Who slew the great wild boar,
The great wild boar that had his den
Amidst the reeds of Cosa's fen,
And wasted fields, and slaughtered men,
　　Along Albinia's shore.

Herminius smote down Aruns:
　　Lartius laid Ocnus low:
Right to the heart of Lausulus
　　Horatius sent a blow.
"Lie there," he cried, "fell pirate!
　　No more, aghast and pale,
From Ostia's walls the crowd shall mark
The track of thy destroying bark.
No more Campania's hinds shall fly
To woods and caverns when they spy
　　Thy thrice accursed sail."

But now no sound of laughter
　　Was heard among the foes.
A wild and wrathful clamor
　　From all the vanguard rose.
Six spears' lengths from the entrance
　　Halted that deep array,
And for a space no man came forth
　　To win the narrow way.

But hark! the cry is Astur:
　　And lo! the ranks divide;
And the great Lord of Luna
　　Comes with his stately stride.
Upon his ample shoulders
　　Clangs loud the four-fold shield,
And in his hand he shakes the brand
　　Which none but he can wield.

He smiled on those bold Romans
　　A smile serene and high;
He eyed the flinching Tuscans,
　　And scorn was in his eye.
Quoth he, "The she-wolf's litter
　　Stand savagely at bay:
But will ye dare to follow,
　　If Astur clears the way?"

Then, whirling up his broadsword
    With both hands to the height,
He rushed against Horatius,
    And smote with all his might.
With shield and blade Horatius
    Right deftly turned the blow.
The blow, though turned, came yet too nigh;
It missed his helm, but gashed his thigh:
The Tuscans raised a joyful cry
    To see the red blood flow.

He reeled, and on Herminius
    He leaned one breathing-space;
Then, like a wild cat mad with wounds,
    Sprang right at Astur's face.
Through teeth, and skull, and helmet,
    So fierce a thrust he sped,
The good sword stood a hand-breadth out
    Behind the Tuscan's head.

And the great Lord of Luna
    Fell at that deadly stroke,
As falls on Mount Alvernus
    A thunder-smitten oak.
Far o'er the crashing forest
    The giant arms lie spread;
And the pale augurs, muttering low,
    Gaze on the blasted head.

On Astur's throat Horatius
    Right firmly pressed his heels,
And thrice and four times tugged amain,
    Ere he wrenched out the steel.
"And see," he cried, "the welcome,
    Fair guests, that waits you here!
What noble Lucomo comes next,
    To taste our Roman cheer?"

But at this haughty challenge
    A sullen murmur ran,
Mingled of wrath, and shame, and dread,
    Along that glittering van.
There lacked not men of prowess,
    Nor men of lordly race;
For all Etruria's noblest
    Were round the fatal place.

Was none who would be foremost
    To lead such dire attack;
But those behind cried "Forward!"
    And those before cried "Back!"
And backward now and forward
    Wavers the deep array;
And on the tossing sea of steel,
To and fro the standards reel;
And the victorious trumpet-peal
    Dies fitfully away.

But meanwhile axe and lever
    Have manfully been plied,
And now the bridge hangs tottering
    Above the boiling tide.
"Come back, come back, Horatius!"
    Loud cried the Fathers all.
"Back, Lartius! back, Herminius!
    Back, ere the ruin fall!"

Back darted Spurius Lartius;
    Herminius darted back:
And, as they passed, beneath their feet
    They felt the timbers crack.
But when they turned their faces,
    And on the farther shore
Saw brave Horatius stand alone,
    They would have crossed once more.

Alone stood brave Horatius,
    But constant still in mind;
Thrice thirty thousand foes before,
    And the broad flood behind.
"Down with him!" cried false Sextus,
    With a smile on his pale face.
"Now yield thee," cried Lars Porsena,
    "Now yield thee to our grace."

Round turned he, as not deigning
    Those craven ranks to see;
Naught spake he to Lars Porsena,
    To Sextus naught spake he:
But he saw on Palatinus
    The white porch of his home;
And he spake to the noble river
    That rolls by the towers of Rome.

"Oh, Tiber! Father Tiber!
    To whom the Romans pray,
A Roman's life, a Roman's arms,
    Take thou in charge this day!"
So he spake, and speaking sheathed
    The good sword by his side,
And with his harness on his back,
    Plunged headlong in the tide.

No sound of joy or sorrow
    Was heard from either bank;
But friends and foes in dumb surprise,
With parted lips and straining eyes,
    Stood gazing where he sank;
And when above the surges
    They saw his crest appear,
All Rome sent forth a rapturous cry,
And even the ranks of Tuscany
    Could scarce forbear to cheer.

But fiercely ran the current,
  Swollen high by months of rain:
And fast his blood was flowing;
  And he was sore in pain,
And heavy with his armor,
  And spent with changing blows:
And oft they thought him sinking,
  But still again he rose.

Never, I ween, did swimmer,
  In such an evil case,
Struggle through such a raging flood
  Safe to the landing-place:
But his limbs were borne up bravely
  By the brave heart within,
And our good Father Tiber
  Bore bravely up his chin.

"Curse on him!" quoth false Sextus:
  "Will not the villain drown?
But for this stay, ere close of day
  We should have sacked the town!"
"Heaven help him!" quoth Lars Porsena,
  "And bring him safe to shore;
For such a gallant feat of arms
  Was never seen before."

And now he feels the bottom;
　　Now on dry earth he stands;
Now round him throng the Fathers
　　To press his gory hands;
And now, with shouts and clapping,
　　And noise of weeping loud,
He enters through the River-gate,
　　Borne by the joyous crowd.

They gave him of the corn-land
　　That was of public right
As much as two strong oxen
　　Could plough from morn till night;
And they made a molten image,
　　And set it up on high,
And there it stands unto this day
　　To witness if I lie.

It stands in the Comitium,
　　Plain for all folk to see;
Horatius in his harness,
　　Halting upon one knee:
And underneath is written,
　　In letters all of gold,
How valiantly he kept the bridge
　　In the brave days of old.

THOMAS BABINGTON MACAULAY

DESIRE

The Indian Serenade

I arise from dreams of thee
In the first sweet sleep of night,
When the winds are breathing low,
And the stars are shining bright
I arise from dreams of thee,
And a spirit in my feet
Hath led me—who knows how?
To thy chamber window, Sweet!

The wandering airs they faint
On the dark, the silent stream—
The champak odors fail
Like sweet thoughts in a dream;
The nightingale's complaint,
It dies upon her heart;
As I must on thine,
Oh, beloved as thou art!

O lift me from the grass!
I die! I faint! I fail!
Let thy love in kisses rain
On my lips and eyelids pale.
My cheek is cold and white, alas!
My heart beats loud and fast;—
Oh! press it to thine own again,
Where it will break at last.

PERCY BYSSHE SHELLEY

I Love You

I love your lips when they're wet with wine
    And red with a wild desire;
I love your eyes when the lovelight lies
    Lit with a passionate fire.
I love your arms when the strands enmesh
    Your kisses against my face.

Not for me the cold, calm kiss
    Of a virgin's bloodless love;
Not for me the saint's white bliss,
    Nor the heart of a spotless dove.
But give me the love that so freely gives
    And laughs at the whole world's blame,
With your body so young and warm in my arms,
    It set my poor heart aflame.

So kiss me sweet with your warm wet mouth,
    Still fragrant with ruby wine,
And say with a fervor born of the South
    That your body and soul are mine.
Clasp me close in your warm young arms,
    While the pale stars shine above,
And we'll live our whole young lives away
    In the joys of a living love.

ELLA WHEELER WILCOX

Faithful to Thee, in
My Fashion

Last night, ah, yesternight, betwixt her lips and mine
    There fell thy shadow, Cynara! thy breath was
        shed
Upon my soul between the kisses and the wine;
        And I was desolate and sick of an old passion,
Yea, I was desolate and bowed my head:
        I have been faithful to thee, Cynara! in my
        fashion.

All night upon mine heart I felt her warm heart beat,
    Night-long within mine arms in love and sleep she
        lay;
Surely the kisses of her bought red mouth were sweet;
        But I was desolate and sick of an old passion,
When I awoke and found the dawn was gray:
        I have been faithful to thee, Cynara! in my
        fashion.

I have forgot much, Cynara! gone with the wind,
     Flung roses, roses riotously with the throng,
Dancing, to put thy pale, lost lilies out of mind;
          But I was desolate and sick of an old passion,
     Yea, all the time, because the dance was long:
          I have been faithful to thee, Cynara! in my
               fashion.

I cried for madder music and for stronger wine,
     But when the feast is finished and the lamps
          expire,
Then falls thy shadow, Cynara! the night is thine;
          And I am desolate and sick of an old passion,
     Yea, hungry for the lips of my desire:
          I have been faithful to thee, Cynara! in my
               fashion.

ERNEST DOWSON

FACING DEATH

Good-Bye

Good-bye, proud world! I'm going home:
Thou art not my friend, and I'm not thine.
Long through thy weary crowds I roam;
A river-ark on the ocean brine,
Long I've been tossed like the driven foam;
But now, proud world! I'm going home.

Good-bye to Flattery's fawning face;
To Grandeur with his wise grimace;
To upstart Wealth's averted eye;
To supple Office, low and high;
To crowded halls, to court and street;
To frozen hearts and hasting feet;
To those who go, and those who come;
Good-bye, proud world! I'm going home.

I am going to my own hearth-stone,
Bosomed in yon green hills alone—
A secret nook in a pleasant land,
Whose groves the frolic fairies planned;
Where arches green, the livelong day,
Echo the blackbird's roundelay,
And vulgar feet have never trod
A spot that is sacred to thought and God.

O, when I am safe in my sylvan home,
I tread on the pride of Greece and Rome;
And when I am stretched beneath the pines,
Where the evening star so holy shines,
I laugh at the lore and the pride of man,
At the sophist schools and the learned clan;
For what are they all, in their high conceit,
When man in the bush with God may meet?

RALPH WALDO EMERSON

I Shall Not Care

When I am dead and over me bright April
   Shakes out her rain-drenched hair,
Though you should lean above me broken-hearted,
   I shall not care.

I shall have peace, as leafy trees are peaceful
   When rain bends down the bough;
And I shall be more silent and cold-hearted
   Than you are now.

SARA TEASDALE

Requiem

Under the wide and starry sky,
Dig the grave and let me lie.
Glad did I live and gladly die,
    And I laid me down with a will.

This be the verse you grave for me:
Here he lies where he longed to be;
Home is the sailor, home from sea,
    And the hunter home from the hill.

ROBERT LOUIS STEVENSON

Crossing the Bar

Sunset and evening star,
    And one clear call for me!
And may there be no moaning of the bar,
    When I put out to sea.

But such a tide as moving seems asleep,
    Too full for sound and foam,
When that which drew from out the boundless deep
    Turns again home.

Twilight and evening bell,
    And after that the dark!
And may there be no sadness of farewell,
    When I embark;

For tho' from out our bourne of Time and Place
    The flood may bear me far,
I hope to see my Pilot face to face
    When I have crost the bar.

ALFRED, LORD TENNYSON

So Live

So live that when thy summons comes to join
The innumerable caravan, which moves
To that mysterious realm, where each shall take
His chamber in the silent halls of death,
Thou go not like the quarry slave at night,
Scourged to his dungeon, but, sustained and soothed
By an unfaltering trust, approach thy grave
Like one who wraps the drapery of his couch
About him, and lies down to pleasant dreams.

(FROM "THANATOPSIS") WILLIAM CULLEN BRYANT

When I Am Dead, My Dearest

When I am dead, my dearest,
    Sing no sad songs for me;
Plant thou no roses at my head,
    Nor shady cypress-tree:
Be the green grass above me
    With showers and dewdrops wet;
And if thou wilt, remember,
    And if thou wilt, forget.

I shall not see the shadows,
    I shall not feel the rain;
I shall not hear the nightingale
    Sing on, as if in pain:
And dreaming through the twilight
    That doth not rise nor set,
Haply I may remember,
    And haply may forget.

CHRISTINA ROSSETTI

Remember

Remember me when I am gone away,
Gone far away into the silent land;
When you can no more hold me by the hand,
Nor I half turn to go, yet turning stay.
Remember me when no more, day by day,
You tell me of our future that you planned;
Only remember me; you understand
It will be late to counsel then or pray.

Yet if you should forget me for a while
And afterwards remember, do not grieve;
For if the darkness and corruption leave
A vestige of the thoughts that once I had,
Better by far you should forget and smile
Than that you should remember and be sad.

CHRISTINA ROSETTI

Death is a Door

Death is only an old door
Set in a garden wall;
On gentle hinges it gives, at dusk
When the thrushes call.

Along the lintel are green leaves,
Beyond the light lies still;
Very willing and weary feet
Go over that sill.

There is nothing to trouble any heart;
Nothing to hurt at all.
Death is only a quiet door
In an old wall.

NANCY BYRD TURNER

He Is Not Dead

I cannot say, and I will not say
That he is dead. He is just away.
With a cheery smile, and a wave of the hand,
He has wandered into an unknown land
And left us dreaming how very fair
It needs must be, since he lingers there.
And you—oh, you, who the wildest yearn
For an old-time step, and the glad return,
Think of him faring on, as dear
In the love of There as the love of Here.
Think of him still as the same. I say,
He is not dead—he is just away.

JAMES WHITCOMB RILEY

The Ballad of Reading Gaol

I never saw a man who looked
    With such a wistful eye
Upon that little tent of blue
    Which prisoners call the sky,
And at every drifting cloud that went
    With sails of silver by.

I walked, with other souls in pain,
    Within another ring,
And was wondering if the man had done
    A great or little thing,
When a voice behind me whispered low,
    "That fellow's got to swing."

Dear Christ! the very prison walls
    Suddenly seemed to reel,
And the sky above my head became
    Like a casque of scorching steel;
And, though I was a soul in pain,
    My pain I could not feel.

I only knew what hunted thought
    Quickened his step, and why
He looked upon the garish day
    With such a wistful eye;
The man had killed the thing he loved,
    And so he had to die.

Yet each man kills the thing he loves,
    By each let this be heard,
Some do it with a bitter look,
    Some with a flattering word,
The coward does it with a kiss,
    The brave man with a sword!

Some kill their love when they are young,
    And some when they are old;
Some strangle with the hands of Lust,
    Some with the hands of Gold:
The kindest use a knife, because
    The dead so soon grow cold.

Some love too little, some too long,
    Some sell, and others buy;
Some do the deed with many tears,
    And some without a sigh:
For each man kills the thing he loves,
    Yet each man does not die.

He does not die a death of shame
    On a day of dark disgrace,
Nor have a noose about his neck,
    Nor a cloth upon his face,
Nor drop feet foremost through the floor
    Into an empty space.

He does not sit with silent men
    Who watch him night and day;
Who watch him when he tries to weep,
    And when he tries to pray;
Who watch him lest himself should rob
    The prison of its prey.

He does not wake at dawn to see
    Dread figures throng his room,
The shivering Chaplain robed in white,
    The Sheriff stern with gloom,
And the Governor all in shiny black,
    With the yellow face of Doom.

He does not rise in piteous haste
    To put on convict-clothes,
While some coarse-mouthed Doctor gloats, and notes
    Each new and nerve-twitched pose,
Fingering a watch whose little ticks
    Are like horrible hammer-blows.

He does not know that sickening thirst
    That sands one's throat, before
The hangman with his gardener's gloves
    Slips through the padded door,
And binds one with three leathern thongs,
    That the throat may thirst no more.

He does not bend his head to hear
    The Burial Office read,
Nor, while the terror of his soul
    Tells him he is not dead,
Cross his own coffin, as he moves
    Into the hideous shed.

He does not stare upon the air
    Through a little roof of glass:
He does not pray with lips of clay
    For his agony to pass;
Nor feel upon his shuddering cheek
    That kiss of Caiaphas.

It is sweet to dance to violins
    When Love and Life are fair:
To dance to flutes, to dance to lutes
    Is delicate and rare:
But it is not sweet with nimble feet
    To dance upon the air!

OSCAR WILDE

In Memoriam

A late lark twitters from the quiet skies;
And from the west,
Where the sun, his day's work ended,
Lingers as in content,
There falls on the old, gray city
An influence luminous and serene,
A shining peace.

The smoke ascends
In a rosy-and-golden haze. The spires
Shine, and are changed. In the valley
Shadows rise. The lark sings on. The sun,
Closing his benediction,
Sinks, and the darkening air
Thrills with a sense of the triumphing night—
Night with her train of stars
And her great gift of sleep.

So be my passing!
My task accomplished and the long day done,
My wages taken, and in my heart
Some late lark singing,
Let me be gathered to the quiet west,
The sundown splendid and serene,
Death.

WILLIAM ERNEST HENLEY

I Have a Rendezvous
with Death

I have a rendezvous with Death
  At some disputed barricade,
    When Spring comes back with rustling shade
      And apple blossoms fill the air—
I have a rendezvous with Death
    When Spring brings back blue days and fair.

It may be he shall take my hand,
And lead me into his dark land,
    And close my eyes and quench my breath—
It may be I shall pass him still.
    I have a rendezvous with Death
On some scarred slope of battered hill,
    When Spring comes round again this year
    And the first meadow flowers appear.

God knows 'twere better to be deep
Pillowed in silk and scented down,
Where Love throbs out in blissful sleep,
Pulse nigh to pulse, and breath to breath,
Where hushed awakenings are dear . . .
But I've a rendezvous with Death
At midnight in some flaming town,
When Spring trips north again this year;
And I to my pledged word am true,
I shall not fail that rendezvous.

ALAN SEEGER

FACING LIFE

Take the World as It Is

Take the world as it is!—with its smiles and its
    sorrow,
    Its love and its friendship—its falsehood and
        truth—
Its schemes that depend on the breath of tomorrow!
    Its hopes which pass by like the dreams of our
        youth—
Yet, oh! whilst the light of affection may shine,
    The heart in itself hath a fountain of bliss!
In the *worst* there's some spark of a nature divine,
    And the wisest and best *take the world as it is.*

CHARLES SWAIN

On His Blindness

When I consider how my light is spent
 Ere half my days in this dark world and wide,
 And that one talent which is death to hide
Lodged with me useless, though my soul more bent
To serve therewith my Maker, and present
 My true account, lest he returning chide,
 "Doth God exact day-labor, light denied?"
I fondly ask. But Patience, to prevent
That murmur, soon replies, "God doth not need
 Either man's work or his own gifts. Who best
 Bear his mild yoke, they serve him best. His state
Is kingly: thousands at his bidding speed,
 And post o'er land and ocean without rest;
 They also serve who only stand and wait."

JOHN MILTON

One Year to Live

If I had but one year to live;
One year to help; one year to give;
One year to love; one year to bless;
One year of better things to stress;
One year to sing; one year to smile;
To brighten earth a little while;
I think that I would spend each day,
In just the very self-same way
That I do now. For from afar
The call may come to cross the bar
At any time, and I must be
Prepared to meet eternity.
So if I have a year to live,
Or just a day in which to give
A pleasant smile, a helping hand,
A mind that tries to understand
A fellow-creature when in need,
'Tis one with me,—I take no heed;
But try to live each day He sends
To serve my gracious Master's ends.

MARY DAVIS REED

High Resolve

I'll hold my candle high, and then
Perhaps I'll see the hearts of men
Above the sordidness of life,
Beyond misunderstandings, strife.
Though many deeds that others do
Seem foolish, rash and sinful too,
Just who am I to criticize
What I perceive with my dull eyes?
I'll hold my candle high, and then,
Perhaps I'll see the hearts of men.

AUTHOR UNKNOWN

The Junk Box

My father often used to say:
"My boy don't throw a thing away:
You'll find a use for it some day."

So in a box he stored up things,
Bent nails, old washers, pipes and rings,
And bolts and nuts and rusty springs.

Despite each blemish and each flaw,
Some use for everything he saw;
With things material, this was law.

And often when he'd work to do,
He searched the junk box through and through
And found old stuff as good as new.

And I have often thought since then,
That father did the same with men;
He knew he'd need their help again.

It seems to me he understood
That men, as well as iron and wood,
May broken be and still be good.

Despite the vices he'd display
He never threw a man away,
But kept him for another day.

A human junk box is this earth
And into it we're tossed at birth,
To wait the day we'll be of worth.

Though bent and twisted, weak of will,
And full of flaws and lacking skill,
Some service each can render still.

EDGAR GUEST

Worthwhile

It is easy enough to be pleasant,
   When life flows by like a song,
But the man worthwhile is one who will smile,
   When everything goes dead wrong.
For the test of the heart is trouble,
   And it always comes with the years,
And the smile that is worth the praises of earth
   Is the smile that shines through tears.

It is easy enough to be prudent,
   When nothing tempts you to stray,
When without or within no voice of sin
   Is luring your soul away;
But it's only a negative virtue
   Until it is tried by fire,
And the life that is worth the honor on earth
   Is the one that resists desire.

By the cynic, the sad, the fallen,
    Who had no strength for the strife,
The world's highway is cumbered today;
    They make up the sum of life.
But the virtue that conquers passion,
    And the sorrow that hides in a smile,
It is these that are worth the homage on earth
    For we find them but once in a while.

ELLA WHEELER WILCOX

A Bag of Tools

Isn't it strange
    That princes and kings,
And clowns that caper
    In sawdust rings,
And common people
    Like you and me
      Are builders for eternity?

Each is given a bag of tools,
    A shapeless mass,
A book of rules;
    And each must make—
Ere life is flown—
    A stumbling block
Or a steppingstone.

R.L. SHARPE

Then Laugh

Build for yourself a strong box,
Fashion each part with care;
When it's strong as your hand can make it,
Put all your troubles there;
Hide there all thought of your failures,
And each bitter cup that you quaff;
Lock all your heartaches within it,
Then sit on the lid and laugh.

Tell no one else its contents,
Never its secrets share;
When you've dropped in your care and worry
Keep them forever there;
Hide them from sight so completely
That the world will never dream half;
Fasten the strong box securely—
Then sit on the lid and laugh.

BERTHA ADAMS BACKUS

FAITH

I Never Saw a Moor

I never saw a moor,
I never saw the sea;
Yet know I how the heather looks,
And what a wave must be.

I never spoke with God,
Nor visited in Heaven;
Yet certain am I of the spot
As if the chart were given.

EMILY DICKINSON

What Thomas an Buile
Said in a Pub

I saw God. Do you doubt it?
   Do you dare to doubt it?
I saw the Almighty Man. His hand
Was resting on a mountain, and
He looked upon the World and all about it:
I saw Him plainer than you see me now,
   You mustn't doubt it.

He was not satisfied;
   His look was all dissatisfied.
His beard swung on a wind far out of sight
Behind the world's curve, and there was light
Most fearful from His forehead, and He sighed,
"That star went always wrong, and from the start
   I was dissatisfied."

He lifted up His hand—
   I say He heaved a dreadful hand
Over the spinning Earth. Then I said, "Stay,
You must not strike it, God; I'm in the way;
And I will never move from where I stand."
He said, "Dear child, I feared that you were dead,"
   And stayed His hand.

JAMES STEPHENS

Faith

I will not doubt, though all my ships at sea
    Come drifting home with broken masts and sails;
    I shall believe the Hand which never fails,
From seeming evil worketh good to me;
    And, though I weep because those sails are
        battered,
    Still will I cry, while my best hopes lie shattered,
        "I trust in Thee."

I will not doubt, though all my prayers return
    Unanswered from the still, white realm above;
    I shall believe it is an all-wise Love
Which has refused those things for which I yearn;
    And though, at times, I cannot keep from
        grieving,
    Yet the pure ardor of my fixed believing
        Undimmed shall burn.

I will not doubt, though sorrows fall like rain,
    And troubles swarm like bees about a hive;
    I shall believe the heights for which I strive,
Are only reached by anguish and by pain;
    And, though I groan and tremble with my crosses,
    I yet shall see, through my severest losses,
            The greater gain.

I will not doubt; well anchored in the faith,
    Like some stanch ship, my soul braves every gale,
    So strong its courage that it will not fail
To breast the mighty, unknown sea of death.
    Oh, may I cry when body parts with spirit,
    "I do not doubt," so listening worlds may hear it
            With my last breath.

ELLA WHEELER WILCOX

A Prayer for Faith

God, give me back the simple faith
    that I so long have clung to,
  My simple faith in peace and hope,
    in loveliness and light—
Because without this faith of mine,
    the rhythms I have sung to
  Become as empty as the sky upon a starless night.

God, let me feel that right is right,
    that reason dwells with reason,
  And let me feel that something grows
    whenever there is rain—
And let me sense that splendid truth
    that season follows season,
  And let me dare to dream
    that there is tenderness in pain.

God, give me back my simple faith
    because my soul is straying
  Away from all the little creeds
    that I so long have known;
Oh, answer me while still I have
    at least the strength for praying,
  For if the prayer dies from my heart
    I will be quite alone.

MARGARET E. SANGSTER

My Church

My church has but one temple,
  Wide as the world is wide,
Set with a million stars,
  Where a million hearts abide.

My church has no creed to bar
  A single brother man
But says, "Come thou and worship"
  To every one who can.

My church has no roof nor walls,
  Nor floors save the beautiful sod—
For fear, I would seem to limit
  The love of the illimitable God.

AUTHOR UNKNOWN. SIGNED E.O.G.

There Is No Unbelief

There is no unbelief;
Whoever plants a seed beneath the sod
And waits to see it push away the clod,
   He trusts in God.

There is no unbelief;
Whoever says, when clouds are in the sky,
"Be patient, heart; light breaketh by and by,"
   Trusts the Most High.

There is no unbelief;
Whoever sees, 'neath winter's field of snow,
The silent harvest of the future grow—
   God's power must know.

There is no unbelief;
Whoever lies down on his couch to sleep,
Content to lock each sense in slumber deep,
   Knows God will keep.

There is no unbelief;
The heart that looks on when dear eyelids close,
And dares to live when life has only woes,
   God's comfort knows.

LIZZIE YORK CASE

Only a Dad

Only a dad with a tired face,
Coming home from the daily race,
Bringing little of gold or fame
To show how well he has played the game;
But glad in his heart that his own rejoice
To see him come and to hear his voice.

Only a dad with a brood of four,
One of ten million men or more
Plodding along in the daily strife,
Bearing the whips and the scorns of life,
With never a whimper of pain or hate,
For the sake of those who at home await.

Only a dad, neither rich nor proud,
Merely one of the surging crowd,
Toiling, striving from day to day,
Facing whatever may come his way,
Silent whenever the harsh condemn,
And bearing it all for the love of them.

Only a dad but he gives his all,
To smooth the way for his children small,
Doing with courage stern and grim
The deeds that his father did for him.
This is the line that for him I pen:
Only a dad, but the best of men.

EDGAR GUEST

Father

Used to wonder just why father
    Never had much time for play,
Used to wonder why he'd rather
    Work each minute of the day.
Used to wonder why he never
    Loafed along the road an' shirked;
Can't recall a time whenever
    Father played while others worked.

Father didn't dress in fashion,
    Sort of hated clothing new;
Style with him was not a passion;
    He had other things in view.
Boys are blind to much that's going
    On about 'em day by day,
And I had no way of knowing
    What became of father's pay.

All I knew was when I needed
    Shoes I got 'em on the spot;
Everything for which I pleaded,
    Somehow, father always got.

Wondered, season after season,
    Why he never took a rest,
And that *I* might be the reason
    Then I never even guessed.

Father set a store on knowledge;
    If he'd lived to have his way
He'd have sent me off to college
    And the bills been glad to pay.
That, I know, was his ambition:
    Now and then he used to say
He'd have done his earthly mission
    On my graduation day.

Saw his cheeks were getting paler,
    Didn't understand just why;
Saw his body growing frailer,
    Then at last I saw him die.
Rest had come! His tasks were ended
    Calm was written on his brow;
Father's life was big and splendid,
    And I understand it now.

EDGAR GUEST

FRIENDSHIP

Love

I love you,
Not only for what you are,
But for what I am
When I am with you.

I love you,
Not only for what
You have made of yourself,
But for what
You are making of me.

I love you
For the part of me
That you bring out;
I love you
For putting your hand
Into my heaped-up heart
And passing over
All the foolish, weak things
That you can't help
Dimly seeing there,
And for drawing out
Into the light
All the beautiful belongings
That no one else had looked
Quite far enough to find.

I love you because you
Are helping me to make
Of the lumber of my life
Not a tavern
But a temple;
Out of the works
Of my every day
Not a reproach
But a song.

I love you
Because you have done
More than any creed
Could have done
To make me good,
And more than any fate
Could have done
To make me happy.

You have done it
Without a touch,
Without a word,
Without a sign.
You have done it
By being yourself.
Perhaps that is what
Being a friend means,
After all.

ROY CROFT

Accept My Full Heart's Thanks

Your words came just when needed.
Like a breeze,
Blowing and bringing from the wide salt sea
Some cooling spray, to meadow scorched with heat
And choked with dust and clouds of sifted sand
That hateful whirlwinds, envious of its bloom,
Had tossed upon it. But the cool sea breeze
Came laden with the odors of the sea
And damp with spray, that laid the dust and sand
And brought new life and strength to blade and
      bloom
So words of thine came over miles to me,
Fresh from the mighty sea, a true friend's heart,
And brought me hope, and strength, and swept away
The dusty webs that human spiders spun
Across my path. Friend—and the word means
      much—
So few there are who reach like thee, a hand
Up over all the barking curs of spite
And give the clasp, when most its need is felt,
Friend, newly found, accept my full heart's thanks.

ELLA WHEELER WILCOX

Confide in a Friend

When you're tired and worn at the close of day
And things just don't seem to be going your way,
When even your patience has come to an end,
Try taking time out and confide in a friend.

Perhaps he too may have walked the same road
With a much troubled heart and burdensome load,
To find peace and comfort somewhere near the end,
When he stopped long enough to confide in a friend.

For then are most welcome a few words of cheer,
For someone who willingly lends you an ear.
No troubles exist that time cannot mend,
But to get quick relief, just confide in a friend.

AUTHOR UNKNOWN

On Friendship

And let your best be for your friend.
If he must know the ebb of your tide, let him know
    its flood also.
For what is your friend that you should seek him with
    hours to kill?
Seek him always with hours to live.
For it is his to fill your need, but not your emptiness.
And in the sweetness of friendship let there be
    laughter, and sharing of pleasures.
For in the dew of little things the heart finds its
    morning and is refreshed.

Your friend is your needs answered.
He is your field which you sow with love and reap
    with thanksgiving.
And he is your board and your fireside.
For you come to him with your hunger, and you seek
    him for peace.

KAHLIL GIBRAN

The Arrow and the Song

I shot an arrow into the air,
It fell to earth, I knew not where;
For, so swiftly it flew, the sight
Could not follow it in its flight.

I breathed a song into the air,
It fell to earth, I knew not where;
For who has sight so keen and strong,
That it can follow the flight of song?

Long, long afterward, in an oak
I found the arrow, still unbroke;
And the song, from beginning to end,
I found again in the heart of a friend.

HENRY WADSWORTH LONGFELLOW

New Friends and Old Friends

Make new friends, but keep the old;
Those are silver, these are gold.
New-made friendships, like new wine,
Age will mellow and refine.
Friendships that have stood the test—
Time and change—are surely best;
Brow may wrinkle, hair grow gray;
Friendship never knows decay.
For 'mid old friends, tried and true,
Once more we our youth renew.
But old friends, alas! may die;
New friends must their place supply.
Cherish friendship in your breast—
New is good, but old is best;
Make new friends, but keep the old;
Those are silver, these are gold.

JOSEPH PARRY

To My Friend

I have never been rich before,
    But you have poured
Into my heart's high door
    A golden hoard.

My wealth is the vision shared,
    The sympathy,
The feast of the soul prepared
    By you for me.

Together we wander through
    The wooded ways.
Old beauties are green and new
    Seen through your gaze.

I look for no greater prize
    Than your soft voice.
The steadiness of your eyes
    Is my heart's choice.

I have never been rich before,
    But I divine
Your step on my sunlit floor
    And wealth is mine!

ANNE CAMPBELL

God Bless You

I seek in prayerful words, dear friend,
    My heart's true wish to send you,
That you may know that, far or near,
    My loving thoughts attend you.

I cannot find a truer word,
    Nor better to address you;
Nor song, nor poem have I heard
    Is sweeter than God bless you!

God bless you! So I've wished you all
    Of brightness life possesses;
For can there any joy at all
    Be yours unless God blesses?

God bless you! So I breathe a charm
    Lest grief's dark night oppress you,
For how can sorrow bring you harm
    If 'tis God's way to bless you?

And so, "through all thy days
    May shadows touch thee never—"
But this alone—God bless thee—
    Then art thou safe forever.

AUTHOR UNKNOWN

There Is Always a Place for You

There is always a place for you at my table,
    You never need to be invited.
I'll share every crust as long as I'm able,
    And know you will be delighted.
There is always a place for you by my fire,
    And though it may burn to embers,.
If warmth and good cheer are your desire
    The friend of your heart remembers!
There is always a place for you by my side,
    And should the years tear us apart,
I will face lonely moments more satisfied
    With a place for you in my heart!

ANNE CAMPBELL

A Poison Tree

I was angry with my friend:
I told my wrath, my wrath did end.
I was angry with my foe:
I told it not, my wrath did grow.

And I watered it in fears
Night and morning with my tears,
And I sunned it with smiles
And with soft deceitful wiles.

And it grew both day and night,
Till it bore an apple bright,
And my foe beheld it shine,
And he knew that it was mine—

And into my garden stole
When the night had veiled the pole;
In the morning, glad, I see
My foe outstretched beneath the tree.

WILLIAM BLAKE

Around the Corner

Around the corner I have a friend,
In this great city that has no end;
Yet days go by, and weeks rush on,
And before I know it a year is gone,
And I never see my old friend's face,
For Life is a swift and terrible race.
He knows I like him just as well
As in the days when I rang his bell
And he rang mine. We were younger then,
And now we are busy, tired men:
Tired with trying to make a name.
"Tomorrow," I say, "I will call on Jim,
Just to show that I'm thinking of him."
But tomorrow comes—and tomorrow goes,
And the distance between us grows and grows
Around the corner!—yet miles away. . . .
"Here's a telegram, sir. . . ."

"Jim died today."

And that's what we get, and deserve in the end:
Around the corner, a vanished friend.

CHARLES HANSON TOWNE

Friendship

Friendship needs no studied phrases,
    Polished face, or winning wiles;
Friendship deals no lavish praises,
    Friendship dons no surface smiles.

Friendship follows Nature's diction,
    Shuns the blandishments of Art,
Boldly severs truth from fiction,
    Speaks the language of the heart.

Friendship favors no condition,
    Scorns a narrow-minded creed,
Lovingly fulfills its mission,
    Be it word or be it deed.

Friendship cheers the faint and weary,
    Makes the timid spirit brave,
Warns the erring, lights the dreary,
    Smooths the passage to the grave.

Friendship—pure, unselfish friendship,
    All through life's allotted span,
Nurtures, strengthens, widens, lengthens,
    Man's relationship with man.

AUTHOR UNKNOWN

Fellowship

When a feller hasn't got a cent
And is feelin' kind of blue,
And the clouds hang thick and dark
And won't let the sunshine thro'
It's a great thing, oh my brethren,
For a feller just to lay
His hand upon your shoulder
    in a friendly sort o' way.

It make a man feel queerish,
It makes the tear-drops start.
And you kind o' feel a flutter
In the region of your heart.
You can't look up and meet his eye,
You don't know what to say
When a hand is on your shoulder
    in a friendly sort o' way.

Oh this world's a curious compound
With its honey and its gall;
Its cares and bitter crosses,
But a good world after all.
And a good God must have made it,
Leastwise that is what I say,
When a hand is on your shoulder
    in a friendly sort o' way.

AUTHOR UNKNOWN

To Know All Is
To Forgive All

If I knew you and you knew me—
If both of us could clearly see,
And with an inner sight divine
The meaning of your heart and mine—
I'm sure that we would differ less
And clasp our hands in friendliness;
Our thoughts would pleasantly agree
If I knew you, and you knew me.

If I knew you and you knew me,
As each one knows his own self, we
Could look each other in the face
And see therein a truer grace.

Life has so many hidden woes,
So many thorns for every rose;
The "why" of things our hearts would see,
If I knew you and you knew me.

NIXON WATERMAN

FULFILLMENT

Today

I have spread wet linen
On lavender bushes,
I have swept rose petals
From a garden walk.
I have labeled jars of raspberry jam,
I have baked a sunshine cake;
I have embroidered a yellow duck
On a small blue frock.
I have polished andirons,
Dusted the highboy,
Cut sweets peas for a black bowl,
Wound the tall clock,
Pleated a lace ruffle . . .
To-day
I have lived a poem.

ETHEL ROMIG FULLER

The Day Is Done

The day is done, and the darkness
   Falls from the wings of Night,
As a feather is wafted downward
   From an eagle in his flight.

I see the lights of the village
   Gleam through the rain and the mist,
And a feeling of sadness comes o'er me
   That my soul cannot resist:

A feeling of sadness and longing,
   That is not akin to pain,
And resembles sorrow only
   As the mist resembles the rain.

Come, read to me some poem,
   Some simple and heartfelt lay,
That shall soothe this restless feeling,
   And banish the thoughts of day.

Not from the grand old masters,
   Not from the bards sublime,
Whose distant footsteps echo
   Through the corridors of Time.

For, like strains of martial music,
   Their mighty thoughts suggest
Life's endless toil and endeavor;
   And tonight I long for rest.

Read from some humbler poet,
   Whose songs gushed from his heart,
As showers from the clouds of summer,
   Or tears from the eyelids start;

Who, through long days of labor,
   And nights devoid of ease,
Still heard in his soul the music
   Of wonderful melodies.

Such songs have power to quiet
 The restless pulse of care,
And come like the benediction
 That follows after prayer.

Then read from the treasured volume
 The poem of thy choice,
And lend to the rhyme of the poet
 The beauty of thy voice.

And the night shall be filled with music,
 And the cares, that infest the day,
Shall fold their tents, like the Arabs,
 And as silently steal away.

HENRY WADSWORTH LONGFELLOW

Thanks Be to God

I do not thank Thee, Lord,
That I have bread to eat while others starve;
Nor yet for work to do
While empty hands solicit Heaven;
Nor for a body strong
While other bodies flatten beds of pain.
No, not for these do I give thanks!

But I am grateful, Lord,
Because my meager loaf I may divide;
For that my busy hands
May move to meet another's need;
Because my doubled strength
I may expend to steady one who faints.
Yes, for all these do I give thanks!

For heart to share, desire to bear
And will to lift,
Flamed into one by deathless Love—
Thanks be to God for this!
Unspeakable! His Gift!

JANIE ALFORD

Better than Gold

Better than grandeur, better than gold,
Than rank and titles a thousandfold,
Is a healthy body and a mind at ease,
And simple pleasures that always please.
A heart that can feel for another's woe,
And share his joys with a genial glow;
With sympathies large enough to enfold
All men as brothers, is better than gold.

Better than gold is a conscience clear,
Though toiling for bread in an humble sphere,
Doubly blessed with content and health,
Untried by the lusts and cares of wealth,
Lowly living and lofty thought
Adorn and ennoble a poor man's cot;
For mind and morals in nature's plan
Are the genuine tests of an earnest man.

Better than gold is a peaceful home
Where all the fireside characters come,
The shrine of love, the heaven of life,
Hallowed by mother, or sister, or wife.
However humble the home may be,
Or tried with sorrow by heaven's decree,
The blessings that never were bought or sold,
And center there, are better than gold.

ABRAM J. RYAN

Life Owes Me Nothing

Life owes me nothing. Let the years
Bring clouds or azure, joy or tears;
   Already a full cup I've quaffed;
   Already wept and loved and laughed,
And seen, in ever-endless ways,
New beauties overwhelm the days.

Life owes me nought. No pain that waits
Can steal the wealth from memory's gates;
   No aftermath of anguish slow
   Can quench the soul fire's early glow.
I breathe, exulting, each new breath,
Embracing Life, ignoring Death.

Life owes me nothing. One clear morn
Is boon enough for being born;
   And be it ninety years or ten,
   No need for me to question when.
While Life is mine, I'll find it good,
And greet each hour with gratitude.

AUTHOR UNKNOWN

A Thankful Heart

Lord, Thou hast given me a cell
  Wherein to dwell,
A little house whose humble roof
  Is weatherproof . . .
Low is my porch as is my fate,
  Both void of state,
And yet the threshold of my door
  Is worn by the poor
Who hither come and freely get
  Good words or meat.
'Tis Thou that crown'st my glittering hearth
  With guileless mirth.
All these and better Thou dost send
  Me to this end,
That I should render for my part
  A thankful heart.

ROBERT HERRICK

Fulfillment

Lo, I have opened unto you the gates of my being,
And like a tide, you have flowed into me.
The innermost recesses of my spirit are full of you
And all the channels of my soul are grown sweet with
      your presence
For you have brought me peace;
    The peace of great tranquil waters,
And the quiet of the summer sea.
    Your hands are filled with peace as
The noon-tide is filled with light;
    About your head is bound the eternal
Quiet of the stars, and in your heart dwells the calm
      miracle of twilight.

I am utterly content.
In all my being is no ripple of unrest
    For I have opened unto you
The wide gates of my being
    And like a tide, you have flowed into me.

AUTHOR UNKNOWN

I Have Found Such Joy

I have found such joy in simple things;
    A plain, clean room, a nut-brown loaf of bread,
A cup of milk, a kettle as it sings,
    The shelter of a roof above my head,
And in a leaf-laced square along the floor,
Where yellow sunlight glimmers through a door.

I have found such joy in things that fill
    My quiet days: a curtain's blowing grace,
A potted plant upon my window sill,
    A rose, fresh-cut and placed within a vase;
A table cleared, a lamp beside a chair,
And books I long have loved beside me there.

Oh, I have found such joys I wish I might
    Tell every woman who goes seeking far
For some elusive, feverish delight,
    That very close to home the great joys are:
The elemental things—old as the race,
Yet never, through the ages, commonplace.

GRACE NOLL CROWELL

GRIEF

She Dwelt Among the Untrodden Ways

She dwelt among the untrodden ways
    Beside the springs of Dove,
A maid whom there were none to praise
    And very few to love:

A violet by a mossy stone
    Half hidden from the eye.
—Fair as a star, when only one
    Is shining in the sky.

She lived unknown, and few could know
    When Lucy ceased to be;
But she is in her grave, and, oh,
    The difference to me!

WILLIAM WORDSWORTH

We Kiss'd Again with Tears

As through the land at eve we went,
And pluck'd the ripen'd ears,
We fell out, my wife and I,
O we fell out I know not why,
And kiss'd again with tears.
And blessings on the falling out
That all the more endears,
When we fall out with those we love,
And kiss again with tears!
For when we came where lies the child
We lost in other years,
There above the little grave,
O there above the little grave,
We kiss'd again with tears.

ALFRED, LORD TENNYSON

O Captain! My Captain!

WRITTEN UPON HEARING OF THE ASSASSINATION
OF PRESIDENT ABRAHAM LINCOLN

O Captain! my Captain! our fearful trip is done,
The ship has weather'd every rack, the prize we
      sought is won,
The port is near, the bells I hear, the people all
      exulting,
While follow eyes the steady keel, the vessel grim and
      daring;
    But O heart! heart! heart!
      O the bleeding drops of red,
         Where on the deck my Captain lies,
         Fallen cold and dead.

O Captain! my Captain! rise up and hear the bells;
Rise up—for you the flag is flung—for you the bugle
      trills,
For you bouquets and ribbon'd wreaths—for you the
      shores a-crowding,
For you they call, the swaying mass, their eager faces
      turning;
    Here Captain! dear father!
      This arm beneath your head!
         It is some dream that on the deck,
         You've fallen cold and dead.

My Captain does not answer, his lips are pale and
    still,
My father does not feel my arm, he has no pulse nor
    will,
The ship is anchor'd safe and sound, its voyage closed
    and done,
From fearful trip the victor ship comes in with object
    won;
    Exult O shores, and ring O bells!
      But I with mournful tread,
        Walk the deck my Captain lies,
          Fallen cold and dead.

WALT WHITMAN

Miss You

I miss you in the morning, dear,
    When all the world is new;
I know the day can bring no joy
    Because it brings not you.
I miss the well-loved voice of you,
    Your tender smile for me,
The charm of you, the joy of your
    Unfailing sympathy.

The world is full of folks, it's true,
    But there was only one of you.

I miss you at the noontide, dear;
    The crowded city street
Seems but a desert now, I walk
    In solitude complete.
I miss your hand beside my own
    The light touch of your hand,
The quick gleam in the eyes of you
    So sure to understand.

The world is full of folks, it's true,
    But there was only one of you.

I miss you in the evening, dear,
    When daylight fades away;
I miss the sheltering arms of you
    To rest me from the day,
I try to think I see you yet
    There where the firelight gleams—
Weary at last, I sleep, and still
    I miss you in my dreams.

The world is full of folks, it's true,
    But there was only one of you.

AUTHOR UNKNOWN

Anthem for Doomed Youth

What passing-bells for these who die as cattle?
Only the monstrous anger of the guns.
Only the stuttering rifles' rapid rattle
Can patter out their hasty orisons.
No mockeries for them; no prayers nor bells,
Nor any voice of mourning save the choirs,—
The shrill, demented choirs of wailing shells;
And bugles calling for them from sad shires.

What candles may be held to speed them all?
Not in the hands of boys, but in their eyes
Shall shine the holy glimmers of good-bys.
The pallor of girls' brows shall be their pall;
Their flowers the tenderness of patient minds,
And each slow dusk a drawing-down of blinds.

WILFRED OWEN

Home They Brought Her Warrior Dead

Home they brought her warrior dead:
    She nor swooned, nor uttered cry:
All her maidens, watching, said,
    "She must weep or she will die."

Then they praised him, soft and low,
    Called him worthy to be loved,
Truest friend and noblest foe;
    Yet she neither spoke nor moved.

Stole a maiden from her place,
    Lightly to the warrior stept,
Took the face-cloth from the face;
    Yet she neither moved nor wept.

Rose a nurse of ninety years,
    Set his child upon her knee—
Like summer tempest came her tears—
    "Sweet my child, I live for thee."

ALFRED, LORD TENNYSON

Annabel Lee

It was many and many a year ago,
    In a kingdom by the sea,
That a maiden there lived whom you may know
    By the name of Annabel Lee;—
And this maiden she lived with no other thought
    Than to love and be loved by me.

She was a child and I was a child,
    In this kingdom by the sea,
But we loved with a love that was more than love—
    I and my Annabel Lee—
With a love that the winged seraphs of Heaven
    Coveted her and me.

And this was the reason that, long ago,
    In this kingdom by the sea,
A wind blew out of a cloud, by night
    Chilling my Annabel Lee;
So that her highborn kinsmen came
    And bore her away from me,
To shut her up in a sepulchre
    In this kingdom by the sea.

The angels, not half so happy in Heaven,
    Went envying her and me:
Yes! that was the reason (as all men know,
    In this kingdom by the sea)
That the wind came out of the cloud, chilling
    And killing my Annabel Lee.

But our love it was stronger by far than the love
    Of those who were older than we—
    Of many far wiser than we—
And neither the angels in Heaven above
    Nor the demons down under the sea,
Can ever dissever my soul from the soul
    Of the beautiful Annabel Lee:—

For the moon never beams without bringing me
    dreams
    Of the beautiful Annabel Lee;
And the stars never rise but I see the bright eyes
    Of the beautiful Annabel Lee;
And so, all the night-tide, I lie down by the side
Of my darling, my darling, my life and my bridge,
    In her sepulchre there by the sea—
    In her tomb by the sounding sea.

EDGAR ALLAN POE

Joseph Rodman Drame

Green be the turf above thee,
    Friend of my better days!
None knew thee but to love thee,
    Nor named thee but to praise.

Tears fell, when thou wert dying,
    From eyes unused to weep,
And long, where thou art lying,
    Will tears the cold turf steep.

When hearts, whose truth was proven,
    Like thine, are laid in earth,
There should a wreath be woven
    To tell the world their worth;

And I, who woke each morrow
    To clasp thy hand in mine,
Who shared thy joy and sorrow,
    Whose weal and woe were thine,

It should be mine to braid it
    Around thy faded brow,
But I've in vain essayed it,
    And feel I cannot now.

While memory bids me weep thee,
    Nor thoughts nor words are free,
The grief is fixed too deeply
    That mourns a man like thee.

FITZ-GREENE HALLECK

Of De Witt Williams on His Way to Lincoln Cemetery

He was born in Alabama.
He was bred in Illinois.
He was nothing but a
Plain black boy.

Swing low swing low sweet sweet chariot.
Nothing but a plain black boy.

Drive him past the Pool Hall.
Drive him past the Show.
Blind within his casket,
But maybe he will know.

Down through Forty-seventh Street:
Underneath the L,
And Northwest Corner, Prairie,
That he loved so well.

Don't forget the Dance Halls—
Warwick and Savoy,
Where he picked his women, where
He drank his liquid joy.

Born in Alabama.
Bred in Illinois.
He was nothing but a
Plain black boy.

Swing low swing low sweet sweet chariot.
Nothing but a plain black boy.

GWENDOLYN BROOKS

Patterns

I walk down the garden-paths,
And all the daffodils
Are blowing, and the bright blue squills.
I walk down the patterned garden-paths
In my stiff, brocaded gown.
With my powdered hair and jeweled fan,
I too am a rare
Pattern. As I wander down
The garden-paths.

My dress is richly figured,
And the train
Makes a pink and silver strain
On the gravel, and the thrift
Of the borders.
Just a plate of current fashion,
Tripping by in high-heeled, ribboned shoes.
Not a softness anywhere about me,
Only whalebone and brocade.
And I sink on a seat in the shade
Of a lime-tree. For my passion
Wars against the stiff brocade.
The daffodils and squills
Flutter in the breeze
As they please.

And I weep;
For the lime-tree is in blossom
And one small flower has dropped upon my bosom.

And the plashing of waterdrops
In the marble fountain
Comes down the garden-paths.
The dripping never stops.
Underneath my stiffened gown
Is the softness of a woman bathing in a marble basin,
A basin in the midst of hedges grown
So thick, she cannot see her lover hiding,
But she guesses he is near,
And the sliding of the water
Seems the stroking of a dear
Hand upon her.
What is Summer in a fine brocaded gown!
I should like to see it lying in a heap upon the
            ground.
All the pink and silver crumpled up on the ground.

I would be the pink and silver as I ran along the
            paths,
And he would stumble after,
Bewildered by my laughter.
I should see the sun flashing from his sword-hilt and
            the buckles on his shoes.
I would choose

To lead him in a maze along the patterned paths,
A bright and laughing maze for my heavy-booted lover.
Till he caught me in the shade,
And the buttons of his waistcoat bruised my body as
      he clasped me,
Aching, melting, unafraid.
With the shadows of the leaves and the sundrops,
And the plopping of the waterdrops,
All about us in the open afternoon—
I am very like to swoon
With the weight of this brocade,
For the sun sifts through the shade.

Underneath the fallen blossom
In my bosom
Is a letter I had hid.
It was brought to me this morning by a rider from the
      Duke.
"Madam, we regret to inform you that Lord Hartwell
Died in action Thursday se'nnight."
As I read it in the white, morning sunlight,
The letters squirmed like snakes.
"Any answer, Madam?" said my footman.
"No," I told him.
"See that the messenger takes some refreshment.
No, no answer."
And I walked into the garden,
Up and down the patterned paths,

In my stiff, correct brocade.
The blue and yellow flowers stood up proudly
        in the sun,
Each one.
I stood upright too,
Held rigid to the pattern
By the stiffness of my grown;
Up and down I walked,
Up and down.

In a month he would have been my husband.
In a month, here, underneath this lime,
We would have broke the pattern;
He for me, and I for him,
He as Colonel, I as Lady,
On this shady seat.
He had a whim
That sunlight carried blessing.
And I answered, "It shall be as you have said."
Now he is dead.

In Summer and in Winter I shall walk
Up and down
The patterned garden-paths
In my stiff, brocaded gown.
The squills and daffodils
Will give place to pillared roses, and to asters,
        and to snow.

I shall go
Up and down
In my gown.
Gorgeously arrayed,
Boned and stayed.
And the softness of my body will be guarded
        from embrace
By each button, hook, and lace.
For the man who should loose me is dead,
Fighting with the Duke in Flanders,
In a pattern called a war.
Christ! What are patterns for?

AMY LOWELL

Home

It takes a heap o' livin' in a house t' make it home,
A heap o' sun an' shadder, an' ye sometimes have t'
    roam
Afore ye really 'preciate the things ye lef' behind,
An' hunger fer 'em somehow, with 'em allus on yer
    mind.
It don't make any differunce how rich ye get t' be,
How much yer chairs an' tables cost, how great yer
    luxury;
It ain't home t' ye, though it be the palace of a king,
Until somehow yer soul is sort o' wrapped round
    everthing.

Home ain't a place that gold can buy or get up in a
    minute;
Afore it's home there's got t' be a heap o' livin' in it;
Within the walls there's got t' be some babies born,
    and then
Right there ye've got t' bring 'em up t' women good,
    an' men;

And gradjerly, as time goes on, ye find ye wouldn't
    part
With anything they ever used—they've grown into yer
    heart:
The old high chairs, the playthings, too, the little
    shoes they wore
Ye hoard; an' if ye could ye'd keep the thumb-marks
    on the door.

Ye've got t' weep t' make it home, ye've got t' sit an'
    sigh
An' watch beside a loved one's bed, an' know that
    Death is nigh;
An' in the stillness o' the night t' see Death's angel
    come,
An' close the eyes o' her that smiled, an' leave her
    sweet voice dumb.
Fer these are scenes that grip the heart, an' when yer
    tears are dried,
Ye find the home is dearer than it was, an' sanctified;
An' tuggin' at ye always are the pleasant memories
O' her that was an' is no more—ye can't escape from
    these.

Ye've got t' sing an' dance fer years, ye've got t' romp
      an' play,

An' learn t' love the things ye have by usin' 'em each
      day;

Even the roses 'round the porch must blossom year by
      year

Afore they 'come a part o' ye, suggestin' someone
      dear

Who used t' love 'em long ago, an' trained 'em jes' t'
      run

the way they do, so's they would get the early
      mornin' sun;

Ye've got t' love each brick an' stone from cellar up t'
      dome:

It takes a heap o' livin' in a house t' make it home.

EDGAR GUEST

No Place to Go

The happiest nights
  I ever know
Are those when I've
  No place to go,
And the missus says
  When the day is through:
"To-night we haven't
  A thing to do."

Oh, the joy of it,
  And the peace untold
Of sitting 'round
  In my slippers old,
With my pipe and book
  In my easy chair,
Knowing I needn't
  Go anywhere.

Needn't hurry
   My evening meal
Nor force the smiles
   That I do not feel,
But can grab a book
   From a near-by shelf,
And drop all sham
   And be myself.

Oh, the charm of it
   And the comfort rare;
Nothing on earth
   With it can compare;
And I'm sorry for him
   Who doesn't know
The joy of having
   No place to go.

                  EDGAR GUEST

Prayer for this House

May nothing evil cross this door,
And may ill fortune never pry
About these windows; may the roar
    And rain go by.

Strengthened by faith, these rafters will
Withstand the batt'ring of the storm;
This hearth, though all the world grow chill,
    Will keep us warm.

Peace shall walk softly through these rooms,
Touching our lips with holy wine,
Til ev'ry casual corner blooms
    Into a shrine.

Laughter shall drown the raucous shout;
And, though these shelt'ring walls are thin,
May they be strong to keep hate out
    And hold love in.

LOUIS UNTERMEYER

Home

Home!
My very heart's desire is safe
Within thy walls;
The voices of my loved ones, friends who come,
My treasured books that rest in niche serene,
All make more dear to me thy haven sweet.
Nor do my feet
Desire to wander out except that they
May have the glad return at eventide—
Dear Home.

Home!
My very heart's contentment lies
Within thy walls.
No worldly calls hath power to turn my eyes
In longing from thy quietness. Each morn
When I go forth upon the duties of the day
I wend my way
Content to know that eve will bring me
Safely to thy walls again.
Dear Home.

NELLIE WOMACK HINES

Home, Sweet Home

'Mid pleasures and palaces though we may roam,
Be it ever so humble, there's no place like home;
A charm from the sky seems to hallow us there,
Which, seek through the world, is ne'er met with
  elsewhere.
 Home, home, sweet, sweet home!
There's no place like home, oh, there's no place like
  home!

An exile from home, splendor dazzles in vain;
Oh, give me my lowly thatched cottage again!
The birds singing gayly, that came at my call—
Give me them—and the peace of mind, dearer than
  all!
 Home, home, sweet, sweet home!
There's no place like home, oh, there's no place like
  home!

I gaze on the moon as I tread the drear wild,
And feel that my mother now thinks of her child,
As she looks on that moon from our own cottage
  door
Thro' the woodbine, whose fragrance shall cheer me
  no more.
  Home, home, sweet, sweet home!
There's no place like home, oh, there's no place like
  home!

How sweet 'tis to sit 'neath a fond father's smile,
And the caress of a mother to soothe and beguile!
Let others delight 'mid new pleasure to roam,
But give me, oh, give me, the pleasures of home,
  Home, home, sweet, sweet home!
There's no place like home, oh, there's no place like
  home!

To thee I'll return, overburdened with care;
The heart's dearest solace will smile on me there;
No more from that cottage again will I roam;
Be it ever so humble, there's no place like home.
  Home, home, sweet, sweet home!
There's no place like home, oh, there's no place like
  home!

JOHN HOWARD PAYNE

A Prayer For A Little Home

God send us a little home,
To come back to, when we roam.

Low walls and fluted tiles,
Wide windows, a view for miles.

Red firelight and deep chairs,
Small white beds upstairs—

Great talk in little nooks,
Dim colors, rows of books.

One picture on each wall,
Not many things at all.

God send us a little ground,
Tall trees stand round.

Homely flowers in brown sod,
Overhead, thy stars, O God.

God bless thee, when winds blow,
Our home, and all we know.

FLORENCE BONE

Home Is Where There Is One To Love Us

Home's not merely four square walls,
Though with pictures hung and gilded;
Home is where Affection calls—
Filled with shrines the Hearth had builded!
Home! Go watch the faithful dove,
Sailing 'neath the heaven above us.
Home is where there's one to love!
Home is where there's one to love us.

Home's not merely roof and room,
It needs something to endear it;
Home is where the heart can bloom,
Where there's some kind lip to cheer it!
What is home with none to meet,
None to welcome, none to greet us?
Home is sweet, and only sweet,
Where there's one we love to meet us!

CHARLES SWAIN

INSPIRATION

Beyond the Profit of Today

Lord, give me vision that shall see
    Beyond the profit of today
Into the years which are to be,
    That I may take the larger, wiser way.

I seek for fortune, Lord, nor claim
    To scorn the recompense I earn;
But help me, as I play the game,
    To give the world its just return.

Thou mad'st the earth for all of us,
  Teach me through struggle, strain and stress
To win and do my share, for thus
  Can profit lead to happiness.

Guard me from thoughts of little men
  Which blind the soul to greater things;
Save me from smug content and then
  From greed and selfishness it brings.

Aid me to join that splendid clan
  Of Business Men who seek to trace
A calm, considered working-plan
  To make the world a better place.

Teach me to hold this task above
  All lesser thoughts within my ken,
That thus I may be worthy of
  The name of Business Man; Amen!

AUTHOR UNKNOWN

Battle-Hymn of the Republic

Mine eyes have seen the glory of the coming of the
      Lord:
He is trampling out the vintage where the grapes of
      wrath are stored;
He hath loosed the fateful lightning of his terrible
      swift sword:
  His truth is marching on.

I have seen him in the watch-fires of a hundred
      circling camps;
They have builded him an altar in the evening dews
      and damps;
I can read his righteous sentence by the dim and
      flaring lamps:
  His day is marching on.

I have read as fiery gospel, writ in burnished rows of
   steel:
"As ye deal with my contemners, so with you my
   grace shall deal;
Let the Hero, born of woman, crush the serpent with
   his heel,
   Since God is marching on."

He has sounded forth the trumpet that shall never call
   retreat;
He is sifting out the hearts of men before his
   judgment-seat:
O, be swift, my soul, to answer him! be jubilant, my
   feet!
   Our God is marching on.

In the beauty of the lilies Christ was born across the
   sea,
With a glory in his bosom that transfigures you and
   me;
As he died to make men holy, let us die to make men
   free,
   While God is marching on.

JULIA WARD HOWE

It Couldn't Be Done

Somebody said that it couldn't be done,
    But he with a chuckle replied
That "maybe it couldn't," but he would be one
    Who wouldn't say so till he'd tried.
So he buckled right in with the trace of a grin
    On his face. If he worried he hid it.
He started to sing as he tackled the thing
    That couldn't be done, and he did it.

Somebody scoffed: "Oh, you'll never do that;
    At least no one ever has done it";
But he took off his coat and he took off his hat,
    And the first thing we knew he'd begun it.
With a lift of his chin and a bit of a grin,
    Without any doubting or quiddit,
He started to sing as he tackled the thing
    That couldn't be done, and he did it.

There are thousands to tell you it cannot be done,
    There are thousands to prophesy failure;
There are thousands to point out to you, one by one,
    The dangers that wait to assail you.
But just buckle in with a bit of a grin,
    Just take off your coat and go to it;
Just start to sing as you tackle the thing
    That "cannot be done," and you'll do it.

EDGAR GUEST

Carry On!

It's easy to fight when everything's right,
And you're mad with the thrill and the glory;
It's easy to cheer when victory's near,
And wallow in fields that are gory.
It's a different song when everything's wrong,
When you're feeling infernally mortal;
When it's ten against one, and hope there is none,
Buck up, little soldier, and chortle:

Carry on! Carry on!
There isn't much punch in your blow.
You're glaring and staring and hitting out blind;
You're muddy and bloody, but never you mind.
Carry on! Carry on!
You haven't the ghost of a show.
It's looking like death, but while you've a breath,
Carry on, my son! Carry on!

And so in the strife of the battle of life
It's easy to fight when you're winning;
It's easy to slave, and starve and be brave,
When the dawn of success is beginning.
But the man who can meet despair and defeat
With a cheer, there's the man of God's choosing;
The man who can fight to Heaven's own height
Is the man who can fight when he's losing.

Carry on! Carry on!
Things never were looming so black.
But show that you haven't a cowardly streak,
And though you're unlucky you never are weak.
Carry on! Carry on!
Brace up for another attack.
It's looking like hell, but—you never can tell:
Carry on, old man! Carry on!

There are some who drift out in the deserts of doubt,
And some who in brutishness wallow;
There are others, I know, who in piety go
Because of a Heaven to follow.
But to labour with zest, and to give of your best,
For the sweetness and joy of the giving;
To help folks along with a hand and a song;
Why, there's the real sunshine of living.

Carry on! Carry on!
Fight the good fight and true;
Believe in your mission, greet life with a cheer;
There's big work to do, and that's why you are here.
Carry on! Carry on!
Let the world be the better for you;
And at last when you die, let this be your cry:
Carry on, my soul! Carry on!

ROBERT SERVICE

Say Not the Struggle Naught Availeth

Say not the struggle naught availeth,
   The labor and the wounds are vain,
The enemy faints not, nor faileth,
   And as things have been they remain.

If hopes were dupes, fears may be liars;
   It may be, in yon smoke conceal'd,
Your comrades chase e'en now the fliers,
   And, but for you, possess the field.

For while the tired waves, vainly breaking,
   Seem here no painful inch to gain,
Far back, through creeks and inlets making,
   Comes silent, flooding in, the main.

And not by eastern windows only,
   When daylight comes, comes in the light;
In front the sun climbs slow, how slowly.
   But westward, look, the land is bright.

ARTHUR CLOUGH

Hold Fast Your Dreams

Hold fast your dreams!
Within your heart
Keep one still, secret spot
Where dreams may go,
And, sheltered so,
May thrive and grow
Where doubt and fear are not.
O keep a place apart,
Within your heart,
For little dreams to go!

Think still of lovely things that are not true.
Let wish and magic work at will in you.
Be sometimes blind to sorrow. Make believe!
Forget the calm that lies
In disillusioned eyes.
Though we all know that we must die,
Yet you and I
May walk like gods and be
Even now at home in immortality.

We see so many ugly things—
Deceits and wrongs and quarrelings;
We know, alas! we know
How quickly fade
The color in the west,
The bloom upon the breast
And youth's blind hour.
Yet keep within your heart
A place apart
Where little dreams may go,
May thrive and grow.
Hold fast—hold fast your dreams!

LOUISE DRISCOLL

Be the Best of Whatever You Are

If you can't be a pine on the top of the hill,
    Be a scrub in the valley—but be
The best little scrub by the side of the rill;
    Be a bush if you can't be a tree.

If you can't be a bust be a bit of the grass,
    And some highway happier make;
If you can't be a muskie than just be a bass—
    But the liveliest bass in the lake!

We can't all be captains, we've got to be crew,
    There's something for all of us here,
There's big work to do, and there's lesser to do,
    And the task you must do is the near.

If you can't be a highway than just be a trail,
    If you can't be the sun be a star;
It isn't by size that you win or you fail—
    Be the best of whatever you are!

DOUGLAS MALLOCH

The New Jerusalem

And did those feet in ancient time
    Walk upon England's mountains green?
And was the Holy Lamb of God
    On England's pleasant pastures seen?

And did the countenance divine
    Shine forth upon our clouded hills?
And was Jerusalem builded here
Among these dark satanic mills?

Bring me my bow of burning gold!
Bring me my arrows of desire!
Bring me my spear! O clouds, unfold!
    Bring me my chariot of fire!

I will not cease from mental fight,
    Nor shall my sword sleep in my hand,
Till we have built Jerusalem
    In England's green and pleasant land.

WILLIAM BLAKE

The Night Has a Thousand Eyes

The night has a thousand eyes,
    And the day but one;
Yet the light of the bright world dies
    With the dying sun.

The mind has a thousand eyes,
    And the heart but one;
Yet the light of a whole life dies
    When love is done.

FRANCIS WILLIAM BOURDILLON

If Love Be Love

In Love, if Love be Love, if Love be ours,
Faith and unfaith can ne'er be equal powers:
Unfaith in aught is want of faith in all.

It is the little rift within the lute,
That by and by will make the music mute,
And ever widening slowly silence all.

The little rift within the lover's lute
Or little pitted speck in garnered fruit,
That rotting inward slowly moulders all.

It is not worth the keeping: let it go:
But shall it? answer, darling, answer, no.
And trust me not at all or all in all.

ALFRED, LORD TENNYSON

Midsummer

You loved me for a little,
   Who could not love me long;
You gave me wings of gladness
   And lent my spirit song.

You loved me for an hour
   But only with your eyes;
Your lips I could not capture
   By storm or by surprise.

Your mouth that I remember
   With rush of sudden pain
As one remembers starlight
   Or roses after rain . . .

Out of a world of laughter
   Suddenly I am sad. . . .
Day and night it haunts me,
   The kiss I never had.

SYDNEY KING RUSSELL

Need of Loving

Folk need a lot of loving in the morning;
 The day is all before, with cares beset—
The cares we know, and they that give no warning;
 For love is God's own antidote for fret.

Folk need a heap of loving at the noontime—
 In the battle lull, the moment snatched from
 strife—
Halfway between the waking and the croon time,
 While bickering and worriment are rife.

Folk hunger so for loving at the nighttime,
 When wearily they take them home to rest—
At slumber song and turning-out-the-light time—
 Of all the times for loving, that's the best.

Folk want a lot of loving every minute—
 The sympathy of others and their smile!
Till life's end, from the moment they begin it,
 Folks need a lot of loving all the while.

STRICKLAND GILLILAN

On Love

When love beckons to you, follow him,
Though his ways are hard and steep.
And when his wings enfold you yield to him.
Though the sword hidden among his pinions may
      wound you.
And when he speaks to you believe in him,
Though his voice may shatter your dreams as the
      north wind lays waste the garden.

For even as love crowns you so shall he crucify you.
      Even as he is for your growth so is he for your
      pruning.
Even as he ascends to your height and caresses your
      tenderest branches that quiver in the sun,
So shall he descend to your roots and shake them in
      their clinging to the earth.

Like sheaves of corn he gathers you unto himself.

He threshes you to make you naked.

He sifts you to free you from your husks.

He grinds you to whiteness.

He kneads you until you are pliant;

And then he assigns you to his sacred fire, that you
       may become sacred bread for God's sacred
       feast.

Love gives naught but itself and takes naught but
       from itself.

Love possesses not nor would it be possessed;

For love is sufficient unto love.

KAHLIL GIBRAN

Give All to Love

Give all to love;
Obey thy heart;
Friends, kindred, days,
Estate, good-fame,
Plans, credit, and the Muse—
Nothing refuse.

'Tis a brave master;
Let it have scope:
Follow it utterly,
Hope beyond hope:
High and more high
It dives into noon,
With wing unspent,
Untold intent;
But it is a god,
Knows its own path,
And the outlets of the sky.

It was not for the mean;
It requireth courage stout,
Souls above doubt,
Valor unbending;
Such 'twill reward—
They shall return
More than they were,
And ever ascending.

Leave all for love;
Yet, hear me, yet,
One word more thy heart behoved,
One pulse more of firm endeavor—
Keep thee today,
Tomorrow, forever,
Free as an Arab
Of thy beloved.

Cling with life to the maid;
But when the surprise,
First vague shadow of surmise
Flits across her bosom young
Of a joy apart from thee,
Free be she, fancy-free;
Nor thou detain her vesture's hem,
Nor the palest rose she flung
From her summer diadem.

Though thou loved her as thyself,
As a self of purer clay,
Though her parting dims the day,
Stealing grace from all alive;
Heartily know,
When half-gods go,
The gods arrive.

RALPH WALDO EMERSON

How Do I Love Thee?

How do I love thee? Let me count the ways.
   I love thee to the depth and breadth and height
   My soul can reach, when feeling out of sight
For the ends of Being and ideal Grace.
I love thee to the level of everyday's
   Most quiet need, by sun and candle-light.
   I love thee freely, as men strive for Right;
I love thee purely as they turn from Praise.

   I love thee with the passion put to use
In my old griefs, and with my childhood's faith.
   I love thee with a love I seemed to lose
With my lost saints,—I love thee with the breath,
   Smiles, tears, of all my life!—and, if God choose,
I shall but love thee better after death.

ELIZABETH BARRETT BROWNING

Believe Me, If All Those Endearing Young Charms

Believe me, if all those endearing young charms,
    Which I gaze on so fondly today,
Were to change by tomorrow, and fleet in my arms,
    Like fairy-gifts fading away,
Thou wouldst still be adored, as this moment thou
       art,
    Let thy loveliness fade as it will,
And around the dear ruin each wish of my heart
    Would entwine itself verdantly still.

It is not while beauty and youth are thine own,
    And thy cheeks unprofaned by a tear,
That the fervour and faith of a soul can be known,
    To which time will but make thee more dear;
No, the heart that has truly loved never forgets,
    But as truly loves on to the close,
As the sunflower turns on her god, when he sets,
    The same look which she turned when he rose.

THOMAS MOORE

All Paths Lead to You

All paths lead to you
    Where e'er I stray,
You are the evening star
    At the end of day.

All paths lead to you
    Hill-top or low,
You are the white birch
    In the sun's glow.

All paths lead to you
    Where e'er I roam.
You are the lark-song
    Calling me home!

BLANCHE SHOEMAKER WAGSTAFF

Forgiven

You left me when the weary weight of sorrow
    Lay, like a stone, upon my bursting heart;
It seemed as if no shimmering tomorrow
    Could dry the tears that you had caused to start.
You left me, never telling why you wandered—
    Without a word, without a last caress;
Left me with but the love that I had squandered,
    The husks of love and a vast loneliness.

And yet if you came back with arms stretched toward me,
    Came back tonight, with carefree, smiling eyes,
And said: "My journeying has somehow bored me,
    And love, though broken, never, never dies!"
I would forget the wounded heart you gave me,
    I would forget the bruises on my soul.
My old-time gods would rise again to save me;
    My dreams would grow supremely new and whole.

What though youth lay, a tattered garment, o'er you?
    Warm words would leap upon my lips, long dumb;
If you came back, with arms stretched out before you,
    And told me, dear, that you were glad to come!

MARGARET E. SANGSTER

When We Two Parted

When we two parted
 In silence and tears,
Half broken-hearted
 To sever for years,
Pale grew thy cheek and cold,
 Colder thy kiss;
Truly that hour foretold
 Sorrow to this.

In secret we met—
 In silence I grieve
That thy heart could forget,
 Thy spirit deceive.
If I should meet thee
 After long years,
How should I greet thee?—
 With silence and tears.

GEORGE GORDON, LORD BYRON

Miss You

Miss you, miss you, miss you;
    Everything I do
Echoes with the laughter
    And the voice of You.

You're on every corner,
    Every turn and twist,
Every old familiar spot
    Whispers how you're missed.

Miss you, miss you, miss you!
    Everywhere I go
There are poignant memories
    Dancing in a row.

Silhouette and shadow
    Of your form and face,
Substance and reality
    Everywhere displace.

Oh, I miss you, miss you!
    God! I miss you, Girl!
There's a strange, sad silence
    'Mid the busy whirl,

Just as tho' the ordinary
    Daily things I do
Wait with me, expectant
    For a word from You.

Miss you, miss you, miss you!
    Nothing now seems true
Only that 'twas heaven
    Just to be with You.

DAVID CORY

When in Disgrace with Fortune and Men's Eyes

When, in disgrace with Fortune and men's eyes,
I all alone beweep my outcast state,
And trouble deaf heaven with my bootless cries,
And look upon myself and curse my fate,
Wishing me like to one more rich in hope,
Featured like him, like him with friends possessed,
Desiring this man's art, and that man's scope,
With what I most enjoy contented least;
Yet in these thoughts myself almost despising,
Haply I think on thee, and then my state,
Like to the lark at break of day arising
From sullen earth, sings hymns at heaven's gate;
   For thy sweet love remembered such wealth brings
   That then I scorn to change my state with kings.

WILLIAM SHAKESPEARE

The Power of the Dog

There is sorrow enough in the natural way
From men and women to fill our day;
And when we are certain of sorrow in store,
Why do we always arrange for more?
Brothers and Sisters, I bid you beware
Of giving your heart to a dog to tear.

Buy a pup and your money will buy
Love unflinching that cannot lie—
Perfect passion and worship fed
By a kick in the ribs or a pat on the head.
Nevertheless it is hardly fair
To risk your heart for a dog to tear.

When the fourteen years which Nature permits
Are closing in asthma, or tumour, or fits,
And the vet's unspoken prescription runs
To lethal chambers or loaded guns,
Then you will find—it's your own affair—
But . . . you've given your heart to a dog to tear.

When the body that lived at your single will,
With its whimper of welcome, is stilled (how still!);
When the spirit that answered your every mood
Is gone—wherever it goes—for good,
You will discover how much you care,
And will give your heart to a dog to tear.

We've sorrow enough in the natural way,
When it comes to burying Christian clay.
Our loves are not given, but only lent,
At compound interest of cent per cent.
Though it is not always the case, I believe,
That the longer we've kept 'em, the more do we
    grieve:
For, when debts are payable, right or wrong,
A short-time loan is as bad as a long—
So why in—Heaven (before we are there)
Should we give our hearts to a dog to tear?

RUDYARD KIPLING

274

MARRIAGE

A Bridge Instead of a Wall

They say a wife and husband, bit by bit,
  Can rear between their lives a mighty wall,
So thick they can not talk with ease through it,
  Nor can they see across, it stands so tall!
Its nearness frightens them but each alone
  Is powerless to tear its bulk away,
And each, dejected, wishes he had known
  For such a wall, some magic thing to say.

So let us build with master art, my dear,
  A bridge of faith between your life and mine,
A bridge of tenderness and very near
  A bridge of understanding, strong and fine—
    Till we have formed so many lovely ties
    There never will be room for walls to rise!

AUTHOR UNKNOWN

On Marriage

You were born together, and together you shall be
    forevermore.
You shall be together when the white wings of death
    scatter your days.
Ay, you shall be together even in the silent memory
    of God.
But let there be spaces in your togetherness,
And let the winds of the heavens dance between you.

Love one another, but make not a bond of love:
Let it rather be a moving sea between the shores of
    your souls.
Fill each other's cup but drink not from one cup.
Give one another of your bread but eat not from the
    same loaf.
Sing and dance together and be joyous, but let each
    one of you be alone,
Even as the strings of a lute are alone though they
    quiver with the same music.

Give your hearts, but not into each other's keeping.
For only the hand of Life can contain your hearts.
And stand together yet not too near together:
For the pillars of the temple stand apart,
And the oak tree and the cypress grow not in each
    other's shadow.

KAHLIL GIBRAN

Prayer of Any Husband

Lord, may there be no moment in her life
When she regrets that she became my wife,
And keep her dear eyes just a trifle blind
To my defects, and to my failings kind!

Help me to do the utmost that I can
To prove myself her measure of a man,
But, if I often fail as mortals may,
Grant that she never sees my feet of clay!

And let her make allowance—now and then—
That we are only grown-up boys, we men,
So, loving all our children, she will see,
Sometimes, a remnant of the child in me!

Since years must bring to all their load of care,
Let us together every burden bear,
And when Death beckons one its path along,
May not the two of us be parted long!

MAZIE V. CARUTHERS

Together

You and I by this lamp with these
Few books shut out the world. Our knees
Touch almost in this little space.
But I am glad. I see your face.
The silences are long, but each
Hears the other without speech.
And in this simple scene there is
The essence of all subtleties,
The freedom from all fret and smart,
The one sure sabbath of the heart.

The world—we cannot conquer it,
Nor change the minds of fools one whit.
Here, here alone do we create
Beauty and peace inviolate;
Here night by night and hour by hour
We build a high impregnable tower
Whence may shine, now and again,
A light to light the feet of men
When they see the rays thereof:
And this is marriage, this is love.

LUDWIG LEWISOHN

Husband and Wife

Whatever I said and whatever you said,
        I love you.
The word and the moment forever have fled;
        I love you.
The breezes may ruffle the stream in its flow,
But tranquil and clear are the waters below;
And under all tumult you feel and you know
        I love you.

Whatever you did and whatever I did,
        I love you.
Whatever is open, whatever is hid,
        I love you.
The strength of the oak makes the tempest a mock,
The anchor holds firm in the hurricane's shock;
Our love is the anchor, the oak and the rock.
        I love you.

Whatever I thought and whatever you thought,
      I love you.
The mood and the passion that made it are naught;
      I love you.
For words, thought and deeds, though they rankle
   and smart,
May never delude us or hold us apart
Who treasure this talisman deep in the heart,
      "I love you."

ARTHUR GUITERMAN

MEMORIES

Jenny Kiss'd Me

Jenny kiss'd me when we met,
    Jumping from the chair she sat in;
Time, you thief, who love to get
    Sweets into your list, put that in!
Say I'm weary, say I'm sad,
    Say that health and wealth have miss'd me,
Say I'm growing old, but add,
    Jenny kiss'd me.

LEIGH HUNT

Break, Break, Break

Break, break, break,
　　On thy cold gray stones, O Sea!
And I would that my tongue could utter
　　The thoughts that arise in me.

O well for the fisherman's boy,
　　That he shouts with his sister at play!
O well for the sailor lad,
　　That he sings in his boat on the bay!

And the stately ships go on
　　To their haven under the hill;
But O for the touch of a vanished hand,
　　And the sound of a voice that is still!

Break, break, break,
　　At the foot of thy crags, O Sea!
But the tender grace of a day that is dead
　　Will never come back to me.

ALFRED, LORD TENNYSON

What Lips My Lips Have Kissed, and Where, and Why

What lips my lips have kissed, and where, and why,
   I have forgotten, and what arms have lain
   Under my head till morning; but the rain
Is full of ghosts tonight, that tap and sigh
Upon the glass and listen for reply,
   And in my heart there stirs a quiet pain
   For unremembered lads that not again
Will turn to me at midnight with a cry.

Thus in the winter stands the lonely tree,
   Nor knows what birds have vanished one by one,
Yet knows its boughs more silent than before:
   I cannot say what loves have come and gone,
I only know that summer sang in me
A little while, that in me sings no more.

EDNA ST. VINCENT MILLAY

Tears, Idle Tears

Tears, idle tears, I know not what they mean,
Tears from the depth of some divine despair
Rise in the heart, and gather to the eyes,
In looking on the happy autumn-fields,
    And thinking of the days that are no more.

Fresh as the first beam glittering on a sail,
That brings our friends up from the underworld,
Sad as the last which reddens over one
That sinks with all we love below the verge;
    So sad, so fresh, the days that are no more.

Ah, sad and strange as in dark summer dawns
The earliest pipe of half-awakened birds
To dying ears, when unto dying eyes
The casement slowly grows a glimmering square;
    So sad, so strange, the days that are no more.

Dear as remembered kisses after death,
And sweet as those by hopeless fancy feigned
On lips that are for others; deep as love,
Deep as first love, and wild with all regret;
    O Death in Life, the days that are no more!

ALFRED, LORD TENNYSON

My Heart Leaps Up

My heart leaps up when I behold
    A rainbow in the sky:
So was it when my life began;
So is it now I am a man;
So be it when I shall grow old,
    Or let me die!
The Child is father of the Man;
And I could wish my days to be
Bound each to each by natural piety.

WILLIAM WORDSWORTH

Remembrance

This memory of my mother stays with me
    Throughout the years: the way she used to stand
    Framed in the door when any of her band
Of children left . . . as long as she could see
Their forms, she gazed, as if she seemed to be
    Trying to guard—to meet some far demand;
    And then before she turned to tasks at hand,
She breathed a little prayer inaudibly.

And now, I think, in some far heavenly place,
    She watches still, and yet is not distressed,
But rather as one who, after life's long race,
    Has found contentment in a well-earned rest,
There, in a peaceful, dreamlike reverie,
She waits, from earthly cares forever free.

MARGARET E. BRUNER

People Liked Him

People liked him, not because
    He was rich or known to fame;
He had never won applause
    As a star in any game.
His was not a brilliant style,
    His was not a forceful way,
But he had a gentle smile
    And a kindly word to say.

Never arrogant or proud,
    On he went with manner mild;
Never quarrelsome or loud,
    Just as simple as a child;
Honest, patient, brave and true:
    Thus he lived from day to day,
Doing what he found to do
    In a cheerful sort of way.

Wasn't one to boast of gold
    Or belittle it with sneers,
Didn't change from hot to cold,
    Kept his friends throughout the years,

Sort of man you like to meet
    Any time or any place.
There was always something sweet
    And refreshing in his face.

Sort of man you'd like to be:
    Balanced well and truly square;
Patient in adversity,
    Generous when his skies were fair.
Never lied to friend or foe,
    Never rash in word or deed,
Quick to come and slow to go
    In a neighbor's time of need.

Never rose to wealth or fame,
    Simply lived, and simply died,
But the passing of his name
    Left a sorrow, far and wide.
Not for glory he'd attained,
    Nor for what he had of pelf,
Were the friends that he had gained,
    But for what he was himself.

EDGAR GUEST

The House on the Hill

They are all gone away,
    The House is shut and still,
There is nothing more to say.

Through broken walls and gray
    The winds blow bleak and shrill;
They are all gone away.

Nor is there one today
    To speak them good or ill:
There is nothing more to say.

Why is it then we stray
 Around that sunken sill?
They are all gone away,

And our poor fancy-play
 For them is wasted skill:
There is nothing more to say.

There is ruin and decay
 In the House on the Hill:
They are all gone away,
There is nothing more to say.

EDWIN ARLINGTON ROBINSON

When the Lamp Is Shattered

When the lamp is shattered,
The light in the dust lies dead;
When the cloud is scattered,
The rainbow's glory is shed;
When the lute is broken,
Sweet tones are remembered not;
When the lips have spoken,
Loved accents are soon forgot.

As music and splendor
Survive not the lamp and the lute,
The heart's echoes render
No song when the spirit is mute:—
No song but sad dirges,
Like the wind through a ruined cell,
Or the mournful surges
That ring the dead seaman's knell.

When hearts have once mingled,
Love first leaves the well-built nest;
The weak one is singled
To endure what it once possessed.
O Love! who bewailest
The frailty of all things here,
Why choose you the frailest
For your cradle, your home, and your bier?

Its passions will rock thee,
As the storms rock the ravens on high;
Bright reason will mock thee,
Like the sun from a wintry sky.
From thy nest every rafter
Will rot, and thine eagle home
Leave the naked to laughter,
When leaves fall and cold winds come.

PERCY BYSSHE SHELLEY

To the Virgins to Make Much of Time

Gather ye rose-buds while ye may,
    Old Time is still a-flying:
And this same flower that smiles today,
    Tomorrow will be dying.

The glorious lamp of heaven, the Sun,
    The higher he's a-getting
The sooner will his race be run,
    And nearer he's to setting.

That age is best which is the first,
    When youth and blood are warmer;
But being spent, the worse, and worst
    Times, still succeed the former.

Then be not coy, but use your time;
    And while ye may, go marry:
For having lost but once your prime,
    You may for ever tarry.

ROBERT HERRICK

MOTHER

A Wonderful Mother

God made a wonderful mother,
A mother who never grows old;
He made her smile of the sunshine,
And He molded her heart of pure gold;
In her eyes He placed bright shining stars,
In her cheeks, fair roses you see;
God made a wonderful mother,
And He gave that dear mother to me.

PAT O'REILLY

Rock Me to Sleep

Backward, turn backward, O Time, in your flight,
Make me a child again just for to-night!
Mother, come back from the echoless shore,
Take me again to your heart as of yore;
Kiss from my forehead the furrows of care,
Smooth the few silver threads out of my hair;
Over my slumbers your loving watch keep—
Rock me to sleep, mother—rock me to sleep!

Backward, flow backward, O tide of the years!
I am so weary of toil and of tears—
Toil without recompense, tears all in vain—
Take them and give me my childhood again!
I have grown weary of dust and decay,
Weary of flinging my soul-wealth away,
Weary of sowing for others to reap—
Rock me to sleep, mother—rock me to sleep!

Tired of the hollow, the base, the untrue,
Mother, O mother, my heart calls for you!
Many a summer the grass has grown green,
Blossomed and faded, our faces between;
Yet, with strong yearning and passionate pain,
Long I to-night for your presence again;
Come from the silence so long and so deep—
Rock me to sleep, mother—rock me to sleep!

Over my heart in the days that are flown,
No love like mother-love ever has shone;
No other worship abides and endures,
Faithful, unselfish, and patient, like yours;
None like a mother can charm away pain
From the sick soul and the world-weary brain;
Slumber's soft calms o'er my heavy lids creep—
Rock me to sleep, mother—rock me to sleep!

Come, let your brown hair, just lighted with gold,
Fall on your shoulders again as of old;
Let it drop over my forehead to-night,
Shading my faint eyes away from the light;
For with its sunny-edge shadows once more,
Haply will throng the sweet visions of yore;
Lovingly, softly, its bright billows sweep—
Rock me to sleep, mother—rock me to sleep!

Mother, dear mother, the years have been long
Since I last listened your lullaby song;
Sing, then, and unto my soul it shall seem
Womanhood's years have been only a dream.
Clasped to your heart in a loving embrace,
With your light lashes just sweeping my face,
Never hereafter to wake or to weep—
Rock me to sleep, mother—rock me to sleep!

ELIZABETH AKERS

Mother

As long ago we carried to your knees
    The tales and treasures of eventful days,
    Knowing no deed too humble for your praise,
Nor any gift too trivial to please,

So still we bring with older smiles and tears,
    What gifts we may to claim the old, dear right;
    Your faith beyond the silence and the night;
Your love still close and watching through the years.

AUTHOR UNKNOWN

The Old Mother

Poor old lady, set her aside—
    Her children are grown, and her work is done;
True, in their service, her locks turned gray,
    But shove her away, unsought, alone.

Give her a home, for decency's sake,
    In some back room, far out of the way,
Where her tremulous voice cannot be heard—
    It might check your mirth when you would be
        gay.

Strive to forget how she toiled for you
    And cradled you oft on her loving breast—
Told you stories and joined your play,
    Many an hour when she needed rest.

No matter for that—huddle her off;
    Your friends might wince at her unwitty jest;
She is too old-fashioned, and speaks so plain—
    Get her out of the way of the coming guest.

Once you valued her cheerful voice,
   Her hearty laugh and her merry song;
But to ears polite they are quite too loud—
   Her jokes too flat, her tales too long.

So, poor old lady, hustle her off—
   In her cheerless room let her sit alone;
She must not meet with your guests tonight,
   For her children are grown and her work is done.

AUTHOR UNKNOWN

Mother's Hands

Dear gentle hands have stroked my hair
    And cooled my brow,
Soft hands that pressed me close
    And seemed to know somehow
Those fleeting moods and erring thoughts
    That cloud my day,
Which quickly melt beneath their suffrage
    And pass away.

No other balm for earthly pain
    Is half so sure,
No sweet caress so filled with love
    Nor half so pure,
No other soul so close akin that understands,
No touch that brings such perfect peace as Mother's
    hands.

W. DAYTON WEDGEFARTH

Concord Hymn

By the rude bridge that arched the flood,
   Their flag to April's breeze unfurled,
Here once the embattled farmers stood,
   And fired the shot heard round the world.

The foe long since in silence slept;
   Alike the conqueror silent sleeps;
And Time the ruined bridge has swept
   Down the dark stream that seaward creeps.

Spirit, that made those heroes dare
   To die, and leave their children free,
Bid Time and Nature gently spare
   The shaft we raise to them and thee.

RALPH WALDO EMERSON

In Flanders Fields

In Flanders fields the poppies blow
Between the crosses, row on row,
    That mark our place; and in the sky
    The larks, still bravely singing, fly
Scarce heard amid the guns below.

We are the Dead. Short days ago
We lived, felt dawn, saw sunset glow,
    Loved and were loved, and now we lie
    In Flanders fields.

Take up our quarrel with the foe:
To you from failing hands we throw
    The torch; be yours to hold it high.
    If ye break faith with us who die
We shall not sleep, though poppies grow
    In Flanders fields.

JOHN McCRAE

The Soldier

If I should die, think only this of me;
    That there's some corner of a foreign field
That is forever England. There shall be
    In that rich earth a richer dust concealed;
A dust whom England bore, shaped, made aware,
    Gave, once, her flowers to love, her ways to
        roam,
A body of England's breathing English air,
    Washed by the rivers, blest by suns of home.

And think, this heart, all evil shed away,
    A pulse in the eternal mind, no less
        Gives somewhere back the thoughts by
           England given;
Her sights and sounds; dreams happy as her day;
    And laughter, learnt of friends; and gentleness,
      In hearts at peace, under an English heaven.

RUPERT BROOKE

America the Beautiful

O beautiful for spacious skies,
 For amber waves of grain,
For purple mountain majesties
 Above the fruited plain!
America! America!
 God shed His grace on thee
And crown thy good with brotherhood
 From sea to shining sea!

O beautiful for pilgrim feet,
 Whose stern, impassioned stress
A thoroughfare for freedom beat
 Across the wilderness!
America! America!
 God mend thine every flaw,
Confirm thy soul in self-control,
 Thy liberty in law!

O beautiful for heroes proved
    In liberating strife,
Who more than self their country loved,
    And mercy more than life!
America! America!
    May God thy gold refine,
Till all success be nobleness
    And every gain divine!

O beautiful for patriot dream
    That sees beyond the years
Thine alabaster cities gleam
    Undimmed by human tears!
America! America!
    God shed His grace on thee,
And crown thy good with brotherhood
    From sea to shining sea!

KATHARINE LEE BATES

The Charge of the
Light Brigade

Half a league, half a league,
  Half a league onward,
All in the valley of Death
Rode the six hundred.
"Forward, the Light Brigade!
Charge for the guns," he said:
Into the valley of Death
  Rode the six hundred.

"Forward, the Light Brigade!"
Was there a man dismay'd?
Not tho' the soldier knew
  Someone had blunder'd:
Theirs not to make reply,
Theirs not to reason why,
Theirs but to do and die:
Into the valley of Death
  Rode the six hundred.

Cannon to right of them,
Cannon to left of them,
Cannon in front of them
  Volley'd and thunder'd;
Storm'd at with shot and shell,
Boldly they rode and well,

Into the jaws of Death,
Into the mouth of Hell
  Rode the six hundred.

Flash'd all their sabers bare,
Flash'd as they turn'd in air
Sabring the gunners there,
Charging an army, while
  All the world wonder'd:
Plung'd in the battery-smoke
Right thro' the line they broke;
Cossack and Russian
Reel'd from the saber-stroke
  Shatter'd and sunder'd.
Then they rode back, but not,
  Not the six hundred.

When can their glory fade?
O the wild charge they made!
  All the world wonder'd.
Honor the charge they made!
Honor the Light Brigade,
  Noble six hundred!

ALFRED, LORD TENNYSON

Breathes There the Man
with Soul So Dead

Breathes there the man, with soul so dead,
Who never to himself hath said,
    This is my own, my native land!
Whose heart hath ne'er within him burn'd
As home his footsteps he hath turn'd,
    From wandering on a foreign strand?
If such there breathe, go, mark him well;
For him no minstrel raptures swell;
High though his titles, proud his name,
Boundless his wealth as wish can claim,—
Despite those titles, power, and pelf,
The wretch, concentred all in self,
Living, shall forfeit fair renown,
And, doubly dying, shall go down
To the vile dust, from whence he sprung,
Unwept, unhonoured, and unsung.

SIR WALTER SCOTT

The Isles of Greece

The isles of Greece! the isles of Greece
   Where burning Sappho loved and sung,
Where grew the arts of war and peace,
   Where Delos rose, and Phoebus sprung!
Eternal summer gilds them yet,
But all, except their sun, is set.

The mountains look on Marathon—
   And Marathon looks on the sea;
And musing there an hour alone,
   I dream'd that Greece might still be free;
For standing on the Persians' grave,
I could not deem myself a slave.

GEORGE GORDON BYRON

PHILOSOPHY

from Evangeline

Talk not of wasted affection! affection never was
    wasted;
If it enrich not the heart of another, its waters,
    returning
Back to their springs, like the rain, shall fill them full
    of refreshment:
That which the fountain sends forth returns again to
    the fountain.

HENRY WADSWORTH LONGFELLOW

Brahma

If the red slayer think he slays,
    Or if the slain think he is slain,
They know not well the subtle ways
    I keep, and pass, and turn again.

Far or forgot to me is near;
    Shadow and sunlight are the same;
The vanished gods to me appear;
    And one to me are shame and fame.

They reckon ill who leave me out;
    When me they fly, I am the wings;
I am the doubter and the doubt,
    And I the hymn the Brahmin sings.

The strong gods pine for my abode,
    And pine in vain the sacred Seven;
But thou, meek lover of the good!
    Find me, and turn thy back on heaven.

RALPH WALDO EMERSON

Happiness

Happiness is like a crystal,
Fair and exquisite and clear,
Broken in a million pieces,
Shattered, scattered far and near.
Now and then along life's pathway,
Lo! some shining fragments fall;
But there are so many pieces
No one ever finds them all.

You may find a bit of beauty,
Or an honest share of wealth,
While another just beside you
Fathers honor, love or health.
Vain to choose or grasp unduly,
Broken is the perfect ball;
And there are so many pieces
No one ever finds them all.

Yet the wise as on they journey
Treasure every fragment clear,
Fit them as they may together,
Imaging the shattered sphere,
Learning ever to be thankful,
Though their share of it is small;
For it has so many pieces
No one ever finds them all.

PRISCILLA LEONARD

Cool Tombs

When Abraham Lincoln was shoveled into the tombs,
    he forgot the copperheads and the assassin . . .
    in the dust, in the cool tombs.

And Ulysses Grant lost all thought of con men and
    Wall Street, cash and collateral turned ashes
    . . . in the dust, in the cool tombs.

Pocahontas' body, lovely as a poplar, sweet as a red
    haw in November or a pawpaw in May, did
    she wonder? does she remember? . . . in the
    dust, in the cool tombs?

Take any streetful of people buying clothes and
    groceries, cheering a hero or throwing confetti
    and blowing tin horns . . . tell me if the lovers
    are losers . . . tell me if any get more than the
    lovers . . . in the dust . . . in the cool tombs.

CARL SANDBURG

Don't Give Up

'Twixt failure and success the point's so fine
Men sometimes know not when they touch the line,
Just when the pearl was waiting one more plunge,
How many a struggler has thrown up the sponge!
Then take this honey from the bitterest cup:
"There is no failure save in giving up!"

AUTHOR UNKNOWN

Stanzas from the Kasidah

Friends of my youth, a last adieu!
    Haply some day we meet again;
Yet ne'er the self-same men shall meet;
    The years shall make us other men:

Fie, fie! you visionary things,
    Ye motes that dance in sunny glow,
Who base and build Eternities
    On briefest moment here below;

Who pass through Life like caged birds,
    The captives of a despot will;
Still wond'ring How and When and Why,
    And Whence and Whither, wond'ring still;

Who knows not Whence he came nor Why,
    Who kens not Whither bound and When,
Yet such is Allah's choicest gift,
    The blessing dreamt by foolish men;

Hardly we learn to wield the blade
    Before the wrist grows stiff and old;
Hardly we learn to ply the pen
    Ere Thought and Fancy faint with cold.

When swift the Camel-rider spans
    The howling waste, by Kismet sped,
And of his Magic Wand a wave
    Hurries the quick to join the dead.

How Thought is impotent to divine
    The secret which the gods defend,
The Why of birth and life and death,
    That Isis-veil no hand may rend.

O the dread pathos of our lives!
    How durst thou, Allah, thus to play
With Love, Affection, Friendship,
    All that shows the god in mortal clay.

Cease, Man, to mourn, to weep, to wail;
  Enjoy thy shining hour of sun;
We dance along Death's icy brink,
  But is the dance less full of fun?

How shall the Shown pretend to ken
  Aught of the Showman or the Show?
Why meanly bargain to believe,
  Which only means thou ne'er canst know?

There is no Good, there is no Bad;
  These be the whims of mortal will:
What works me weal that call I "good,"
  What harms and hurts I hold as "ill:"

They change with place, they shift with race;
  And, in the veriest span of Time,
Each Vice has won a Virtue's crown;
  All good was banned as Sin or Crime:

All Faith is false, all Faith is true:
    Truth is the shattered mirror strown
In myriad bits; while each believes
    His little bit the whole to own.

What is the Truth? was askt of yore.
    Reply all object Truth is one
As twain of halves aye makes as whole;
    The moral Truth for all is none.

With God's foreknowledge man's free will!
    What monster-growth of human brain,
What powers of light shall ever pierce
    This puzzle dense with words inane?

There is no Heaven, there is no Hell;
    These be the dreams of baby minds;
Tools of the wily Fetisheer,
    To 'fright the fools his cunning blinds.

Who drinks one bowl hath scant delight;
　　To poorest passion he was born;
Who drains the score must e'er expect
　　To rue the headache of the morn.

From self-approval seek applause:
　　What ken not men thou kennest, thou!
Spurn ev'ry idol others raise:
　　Before thine own Ideal bow:

Be thine own Deus: Make self free,
　　Liberal as the circling air:
Thy Thought to thee an Empire be;
　　Break every prisoning lock and bar:

SIR RICHARD F. BURTON

Ozymandias

I met a traveler from an antique land,
Who said: Two vast and trunkless legs of stone
Stand in the desert. Near them, on the sand,
Half sunk, a shattered visage lies, whose frown,
And wrinkled lip, and sneer of cold command,
Tell that its sculptor well those passions read,
Which yet survive, stamped on these lifeless things,
The hand that mocked them, and the heart that fed:
And on the pedestal these words appear:
"My name is Ozymandias, King of Kings:
Look on my works, ye Mighty, and despair!"
Nothing beside remains. Round the decay
Of that colossal wreck, boundless and bare
The lone and level sands stretch far away.

PERCY BYSSHE SHELLEY

The World Is Too Much With Us

The world is too much with us; late and soon,
Getting and spending, we lay waste our powers:
Little we see in Nature that is ours;
We have given our hearts away, a sordid boon!
The sea that bares her bosom to the moon;
The winds that will be howling at all hours,
And are up-gathered now like sleeping flowers;
For this, for everything, we are out of tune;
It moves us not.—Great God! I'd rather be
A pagan suckled in a creed outworn.
So might I, standing on this pleasant lea,
Have glimpses that would make me less forlorn;
Have sight of Proteus rising from the sea;
Or hear old Triton blow his wreathed horn.

WILLIAM WORDSWORTH

Vitae Summa Brevis

They are not long, the weeping and the laughter,
   Love and desire and hate;
I think they have no portion in us after
    We pass the gate.

They are not long, the days of wine and roses:
   Out of a misty dream
Our path emerges for a while, then closes
    Within a dream.

ERNEST DOWSON

Ulysses

It little profits that an idle king,
By this still hearth, among these barren crags,
Matched with an aged wife, I mete and dole
Unequal laws unto a savage race,
That hoard, and sleep, and feed, and know not me.
I cannot rest from travel: I will drink
Life to the lees: all times I have enjoyed
Greatly, have suffered greatly, both with those
That loved me, and alone; on shore, and when
Through scudding drifts the rainy Hyades
Vext the dim sea. I am become a name;
For always roaming with a hungry heart
Much have I seen and known: cities of men
And manners, climates, councils, governments,
Myself not least, but honored of them all,—
And drunk delight of battle with my peers,
Far on the ringing plains of windy Troy.
I am a part of all that I have met;
Yet all experience is an arch wherethrough
Gleams that untraveled world, whose margin fades
For ever and for ever when I move.
How dull it is to pause, to make an end,

To rust unburnished, not to shine in use!
As though to breathe were life. Life piled on life
Were all too little, and of one to me
Little remains: but every hour is saved
From that eternal silence, something more,
A bringer of new things; and vile it were
For some three suns to store and hoard myself,
And this gray spirit yearning in desire
To follow knowledge, like a sinking star,
Beyond the utmost bound of human thought.

    This is my son, mine own Telemachus,
To whom I leave the scepter and the isle—
Well-loved of me, discerning to fulfill
This labor, by slow prudence to make mild
A rugged people, and through soft degrees
Subdue them to the useful and the good.
Most blameless is he, centered in the sphere
Of common duties, decent not to fail
In offices of tenderness, and pay
Meet adoration to my household gods,
When I am gone. He works his work, I mine.

There lies the port: the vessel puffs her sail:
There gloom the dark broad seas. My mariners,
Souls that have toiled, and wrought, and thought
        with me—
That ever with a frolic welcome took
The thunder and the sunshine, and opposed
Free hearts, free foreheads—you and I are old;
Old age hath yet his honor and his toil;
Death closes all: but something ere the end,
Some work of noble note, may yet be done,
Not unbecoming men that strove with Gods.
The lights begin to twinkle from the rocks:
The long day wanes: the slow moon climbs: the deep
Moans round with many voices. Come, my friends,
'Tis not too late to seek a newer world.
Push off, and sitting well in order smite
The sounding furrows; for my purpose holds
To sail beyond the sunset, and the baths
Of all the western stars, until I die.
It may be that the gulfs will wash us down:
It may be we shall touch the Happy Isles,

And see the great Achilles, whom we knew.
Though much is taken, much abides; and though
We are not now that strength which in old days
Moved earth and heaven, that which we are, we
      are,—
One equal temper of heroic hearts,
Made weak by time and fate, but strong in will
To strive, to seek, to find, and not to yield.

ALFRED, LORD TENNYSON

Money

When I had money, money, O!
    I knew no joy till I went poor;
For many a false man as a friend
    Came knocking all day at my door.

Then felt I like a child that holds
    A trumpet that he must not blow
Because a man is dead; I dared
    Not speak to let this false world know.

Much have I thought of life, and seen
    How poor men's hearts are ever light;
And how their wives do hum like bees
    About their work from morn till night.

So, when I hear these poor ones laugh,
    And see the rich ones coldly frown—
Poor men, think I, need not go up
    So much as rich men should come down.

When I had money, money, O!
    My many friends proved all untrue;
But now I have no money, O!
    My friends are real, though very few.

WILLIAM HENRY DAVIES

Ode

We are the music-makers,
    And we are the dreamers of dreams,
Wandering by lone sea-breakers,
    And sitting by desolate streams;
World-losers and world-forsakers,
    On whom the pale moon gleams:
Yet we are the movers and shakers
    Of the world for ever, it seems.

With wonderful deathless ditties
We build up the world's cities,
    And out of a fabulous story
    We fashion an empire's glory:
One man with a dream, at pleasure,
    Shall go forth and conquer a crown;
And three with a new song's measure
    Can trample an empire down.

We, in the ages lying
   In the buried past of the earth,
Built Nineveh with our sighing,
   And Babel itself with our mirth;
And o'erthrew them with prophesying
   To the old of the new world's worth;
For each age is a dream that is dying,
   Or one that is coming to birth.

ARTHUR O'SHAUGHNESSY

PRAYER

For a New Home

Oh, love this house, and make of it a Home—
A cherished, hallowed place.
Root roses at its base, and freely paint
The glow of welcome on its smiling face!
For after friends are gone, and children marry,
And you are left alone . . .
The house you loved will clasp you to its heart,
Within its arms of lumber and of stone.

ROSA ZAGNONI MARINONI

Recessional

God of our fathers, known of old—
    Lord of our far-flung battle-line—
Beneath whose awful Hand we hold
    Dominion over palm and pine—
Lord God of Hosts, be with us yet,
Lest we forget, lest we forget!

The tumult and the shouting dies—
    The captains and the kings depart—
Still stands Thine ancient sacrifice,
    An humble and a contrite heart.
Lord God of Hosts, be with us yet,
Lest we forget, lest we forget!

Far-call'd our navies melt away—
    On dune and headland sinks the fire—
Lo, all our pomp of yesterday
    Is one with Nineveh and Tyre!
Judge of the Nations, spare us yet,
Lest we forget, lest we forget!

If, drunk with sight of power, we loose
    Wild tongues that have not Thee in awe—
Such boasting as the Gentiles use
    Or lesser breeds without the Law—
Lord God of Hosts, be with us yet,
Lest we forget, lest we forget!

For heathen heart that puts her trust
    In reeking tube and iron shard—
All valiant dust that builds on dust,
    And guarding calls not Thee to guard—
For frantic boast and foolish word,
Thy Mercy on Thy People, Lord!

RUDYARD KIPLING

My Evening Prayer

If I have wounded any soul to-day,
If I have caused one foot to go astray,
If I have walked in my own wilful way—
    Good Lord, forgive!

If I have uttered idle words or vain,
If I have turned aside from want or pain,
Lest I myself should suffer through the strain—
    Good Lord, forgive!

If I have craved for joys that are not mine,
If I have let my wayward heart repine,
Dwelling on things of earth, not things divine—
    Good Lord, forgive!

If I have been perverse, or hard, or cold,
If I have longed for shelter in Thy fold,
When Thou hast given me some part to hold—
    Good Lord, forgive.

Forgive the sins I have confessed to Thee,
Forgive the secret sins I do not see,
That which I know not, Father, teach Thou me—
    Help me to live.

CHARLES H. GABRIEL

A Prayer

Let me do my work each day;
And if the darkened hours of despair overcome me,
May I not forget the strength that comforted me
In the desolation of other times.
May I still remember the bright hours that found me
Walking over the silent hills of my childhood,
Or dreaming on the margin of the quiet river,
When a light glowed within me,
And I promised my early God to have courage
Amid the tempests of the changing years.
Spare me from bitterness
And from the sharp passions of unguarded moments.
May I not forget that poverty and riches are of the
      spirit.
Though the world know me not,
May my thoughts and actions be such
As shall keep me friendly with myself.
Lift my eyes from the earth,
And let me not forget the uses of the stars.

Forbid that I should judge others,
Lest I condemn myself.
Let me not follow the clamor of the world,
But walk calmly in my path.
Give me a few friends who will love me for what I
    am;
And keep ever burning before my vagrant steps
The kindly light of hope.
And though age and infirmity overtake me,
And I come not within sight of the castle of my
    dreams,
Teach me still to be thankful for life,
And for time's olden memories that are good and
    sweet;
And may the evening's twilight find me gentle still.

MAX EHRMANN

Prayer

God, though this life is but a wraith,
  Although we know not what we use,
Although we grope with little faith,
  Give me the heart to fight—and lose.

Ever insurgent let me be,
  Make me more daring than devout;
From sleek contentment keep me free,
  And fill me with a buoyant doubt.

Open my eyes to visions girt
  With beauty, and with wonder lit—
But let me always see the dirt,
  And all that spawn and die in it.

Open my ears to music; let
  Me thrill with Spring's first flutes and drums—
But never let me dare forget
  The bitter ballads of the slums.

From compromise and things half-done,
  Keep me, with stern and stubborn pride.
And when, at last, the fight is won,
  God, keep me still unsatisfied.

LOUIS UNTERMEYER

A Prayer for Every Day

Make me too brave to lie or be unkind.
Make me too understanding, too, to mind
The little hurts companions give, and friends,
The careless hurts that no one quite intends.
Make me too thoughtful to hurt others so.
Help me to know
The inmost hearts of those for whom I care,
Their secret wishes, all the loads they bear,
That I may add my courage to their own.
May I make lonely folks feel less alone,
And happier ones a little happier yet.
May I forget
What ought to be forgotten; and recall,
Unfailing, all
That ought to be recalled, each kindly thing,
Forgetting what might sting.
To all upon my way,
Day after day,
Let me be joy, be hope! Let my life sing!

MARY CAROLYN DAVIES

Morning Prayer

When little things would irk me, and I grow
Impatient with my dear one, make me know
How in a moment joy can take its flight
And happiness be quenched in endless night.
Keep this thought with me all the livelong day
That I may guard the harsh words I might say
When I would fret and grumble, fiery hot,
At trifles that tomorrow are forgot—
Let me remember, Lord, how it would be
If these, my loved ones, were not here with me.

ELLA WHEELER WILCOX

A Prayer Found in Chester Cathedral

Give me a good digestion, Lord
    And also something to digest;
Give me a healthy body, Lord,
    With sense to keep it at its best.

Give me a healthy mind, good Lord,
    To keep the good and pure in sight;
Which, seeing sin, is not appalled,
    But finds a way to set it right.

Give me a mind that is not bored,
    That does not whimper, whine or sigh;
Don't let me worry overmuch
    About the fussy thing called "I."

Give me a sense of humor, Lord,
    Give me the grace to see a joke;
To get some happiness from life,
    And pass it on to other folk.

AUTHOR UNKNOWN

A Morning Prayer

Let me today do something that will take
    A little sadness from the world's vast store,
And may I be so favored as to make
    Of joy's too scanty sum a little more.

Let me not hurt, by any selfish deed
    Or thoughtless word, the heart of foe or friend,
Nor would I pass unseeing worthy need,
    Or sin by silence when I should defend.

However meager by my worldly wealth,
    Let me give something that shall aid my kind—
A word of courage, or a thought of health
    Dropped as I pass for troubled hearts to find.

Let me tonight look back across the span
    Twixt dawn and dark, and to my conscience
      say—
Because of some good act to beast or man—
    "The world is better that I lived today."

ELLA WHEELER WILCOX

A Wise Old Owl

A wise old owl lived in an oak;
The more he saw the less he spoke;
The less he spoke the more he heard:
Why can't we all be like that bird?

UNKNOWN

To a Fat Lady Seen From the Train

O why do you walk through the fields in gloves,
    Missing so much and so much?
O fat white woman, whom nobody loves,
Why do you walk through the fields in gloves,
When the grass is soft as the breast of doves
    And shivering-sweet to the touch?
O why do you walk through the fields in gloves,
    Missing so much and so much?

FRANCES CORNFORD

Get a Transfer

If you are on the Gloomy Line,
    Get a transfer.
If you're inclined to fret and pine,
    Get a transfer.
Get off the track of doubt and gloom,
Get on the Sunshine Track—there's room—
    Get a transfer.

If you're on the Worry Train,
    Get a transfer.
You must not stay there and complain,
    Get a transfer.
The Cheerful Cars are passing through,
And there's lots of room for you—
    Get a transfer.

If you're on the Grouchy Track,
    Get a transfer.
Just take a Happy Special back,
    Get a transfer.
Jump on the train and pull the rope,
That lands you at the station Hope—
    Get a transfer.

AUTHOR UNKNOWN

At Set of Sun

If you sit down at set of sun
And count the acts that you have done,
    And, counting, find
One self-denying deed, one word
That eased the heart of him who heard—
    One glance most kind,
That fell like sunshine where it went—
Then you may count that day well spent.

But, if, through all the livelong day,
You've cheered no heart, by yea or nay—
    If, through it all
You've nothing done that you can trace
That brought the sunshine to one face—
    No act most small
That helped some soul and nothing cost—
Then count that day as worse than lost.

GEORGE ELIOT

Grass

Pile the bodies high at Austerlitz and Waterloo.
Shovel them under and let me work—
  I am the grass; I cover all.

And pile them high at Gettysburg
And pile them high at Ypres and Verdun.
Shovel them under and let me work.
Two years, ten years, and passengers ask the
    conductor:
  What place is this?
  Where are we now?

  I am the grass.
  Let me work.

CARL SANDBURG

stanzas from the Rubaiyat of Omar Khayyam

Come, fill the Cup, and in the fire of Spring
Your Winter-garment of Repentance fling:
   The Bird of Time has but a little way
To flutter—and the Bird is on the Wing.

Whether at Naishapur or Babylon,
Whether the Cup with sweet or bitter run,
   The Wine of Life keeps oozing drop by drop,
The Leaves of Life keep falling one by one.

A Book of Verses underneath the Bough,
A Jug of Wine, a Loaf of Bread—and Thou
   Beside me singing in the Wilderness—
O, Wilderness were Paradise enow!

Some for the Glories of This World; and some
Sigh for the Prophet's Paradise to come;
   Ah, take he Cash, and let the Credit go,
Nor heed the rumble of a distant Drum!

Ah, my Beloved, fill the Cup that clears
To-day of past Regrets and future Fears;
   To-morrow!—Why, To-morrow I may be
Myself with Yesterday's Sev'n thousand Years.

For some we loved, the loveliest and the best
That from his Vintage rolling Time hath prest,
  Have drunk their Cup a Round or two before.
And one by one crept silently to rest.

Ah, make the most of what we yet may spend,
Before we too into the Dust descend;
  Dust into Dust, and under Dust to lie,
Sans Wine, sans Song, sans Singer, and— sans End!

And if the Wine you drink, the Lip you press,
End in what All begins and ends in—Yes;
  Think then you are To-day what Yesterday
You were—To-morrow you shall not be less.

When You and I behind the Veil are past,
Oh, but the long, long while the World shall last
  Which of our Coming and Departure heeds
As the Sea's self should heed a pebble cast.

The Moving Finger writes; and, having writ,
Moves on: nor all your Piety nor Wit
  Shall lure it back to cancel half a Line,
Nor all your Tears wash out a Word of it.

And that inverted Bowl they call the Sky,
Whereunder crawling coop'd we live and die,
  Lift not your hands to *It* for help—for It
As impotently moves as you or I.

Oh Thou, who didst with pitfall and with gin
Beset the Road I was to wander in,
  Thou wilt not with Predestined Evil round
Enmesh, and then impute my Fall to Sin!

Oh Thou, who Man of baser Earth didst make,
And ev'n with paradise devise the Snake;
  For all the Sin wherewith the Face of Man
Is blacken'd—Man's forgiveness give—and take!

Indeed, indeed, Repentance oft before
I swore—but was I sober when I swore!
  And then and then came Spring, and Rose- in-hand
My thread-bare Penitence apieces tore.

Ah Love! could you and I with Him conspire
To grasp this sorry Scheme of Things Entire,
  Would not we shatter it to bits—and then
Re-mould it nearer to the Heart's desire! . . .

EDWARD FITZGERALD

Who Hath a Book

Who hath a book
   Has friends at hand,
And gold and gear
   At his command;

And rich estates,
   If he but look,
Are held by him
   Who hath a book.

Who hath a book
   Has but to read
And he may be
   A king indeed;

His Kingdom is
   His inglenook;
All this is his
   Who hath a book.

WILBUR D. NESBIT

Elegy Written in a
Country Churchyard

The curfew tolls the knell of parting day,
   The lowing herd winds slowly o'er the lea,
The plowman homeward plods his weary way,
   And leaves the world to darkness and to me.

Now fades the glimmering landscape on the sight,
   And all the air a solemn stillness holds,
Save where the beetle wheels his droning flight,
   And drowsy tinklings lull the distant folds;

Save that from yonder ivy-mantled tow'r
   The moping owl does to the moon complain
Of such, as wand'ring near her secret bow'r,
   Molest her ancient solitary reign.

Beneath those rugged elms, that yew-tree's shade,
   Where leaves the turf in many a mould'ring heap,
Each in his narrow cell for ever laid,
   The rude Forefathers of the hamlet sleep.

The breezy call of incense-breathing Morn,
　The swallow twittering from the straw-built shed,
The cock's shrill clarion, or the echoing horn,
　No more shall rouse them from their lowly bed.

For them no more the blazing hearth shall burn,
　Or busy housewife ply her evening care:
No children run to lisp their sire's return,
　Or climb his knees the envied kiss to share.

Oft did the harvest to their sickle yield,
　Their furrow oft the stubborn glebe has broke:
How jocund did they drive their team afield!
　How bow'd the woods beneath their sturdy
　　stroke!

Let not Ambition mock their useful toil,
　Their homely joys, and destiny obscure;
Nor Grandeur hear with a disdainful smile,
　The short and simple annals of the poor.

The boast of heraldry, the pomp of pow'r,
　And all that beauty, all that wealth e'er gave,
Awaits alike th' inevitable hour:
　The paths of glory lead but to the grave.

Nor you, ye proud, impute to these the fault,
    If Memory o'er their tomb no trophies raise.
Where through the long-drawn aisle and fretted
    vault
    The pealing anthem swells the note of praise.

Can storied urn or animated bust
    Back to its mansion call the fleeting breath?
Can Honour's voice provoke the silent dust,
    Or Flatt'ry soothe the dull cold ear of death?

Perhaps in this neglected spot is laid
    Some heart once pregnant with celestial fire;
Hands that the rod of empire might have sway'd
    Or waked to ecstasy the living lyre.

But Knowledge to their eyes her ample page
    Rich with the spoils of time did ne'er unroll;
Chill Penury repress'd their noble rage,
    And froze the genial current of the soul.

Full many a gem of purest ray serene,
    The dark unfathom'd caves of ocean bear:
Full many a flower is born to blush unseen,
    And waste its sweetness on the desert air.

Some village Hampden that with dauntless breast
   The little tyrant of his fields withstood;
Some mute inglorious Milton here may rest,
   Some Cromwell guiltless of his country's blood.

Th' applause of list'ning senates to command,
   The threats of pain and ruin to despise,
To scatter plenty o'er a smiling land,
   And read their history in a nation's eyes,

Their lot forbade: nor circumscribed alone
   Their growing virtues, but their crimes confined;
Forbade to wade through slaughter to a throne,
   And shut the gates of mercy on mankind.

The struggling pangs of conscious truth to hide,
   To quench the blushes of ingenuous shame,
Or heap the shrine of Luxury and Pride
   With incense kindled at the Muse's flame.

Far from the madding crowd's ignoble strife,
   Their sober wishes never learn'd to stray;
Along the cool sequester'd vale of life
   They kept the noiseless tenor of their way.

Yet ev'n these bones from insult to protect,
  Some frail memorial still erected nigh,
With uncouth rhymes and shapeless scuplture deck't,
  Implores the passing tribute of a sigh.

Their name, their years, spelt by th' unletter'd Muse,
  The place of fame and elegy supply:
And many a holy text around she strews,
  That teach the rustic moralist to die.

For who, to dumb Forgetfulness a prey,
  This pleasing anxious being e'er resign'd,
Left the warm precincts of the cheerful day,
  Nor cast one longing lingering look behind?

On some fond breast the parting soul relies,
  Some pious drops the closing eye requires;
E'en from the tomb the voice of Nature cries,
  E'en in our ashes live their wonted fires.

For thee, who, mindful of th' unhonour'd dead,
  Dost in these lines their artless tale relate;
If chance, by lonely contemplation led,
  Some kindred spirit shall inquire thy fate,

Haply some hoary-headed swain may say,
"Oft have we seen him at the peep of dawn
Brushing with hasty steps the dews away
To meet the sun upon the upland lawn.

"There at the foot of yonder nodding beech
That wreathes its old fantastic roots so high,
His listless length at noontide would he stretch,
And pore upon the brook that babbles by.

"Hard by yon wood, now smiling as in scorn,
Muttering his wayward fancies he would rove;
Now drooping, woeful-wan, like one forlorn,
Or crazed with care, or cross'd in hopeless love.

"One morn I miss'd him on the custom'd hill,
Along the heath, and near his fav'rite tree;
Another came, nor yet beside the rill,
Nor up the lawn, nor at the wood was he;

"The next, with dirges due in sad array
Slow through the church-way path we saw him borne,
Approach and read (for thou canst read) the lay
Graved on the stone beneath yon aged thorn."

THE EPITAPH

Here rests his head upon the lap of earth
  A youth to Fortune and to Fame unknown.
Fair Science frown'd not on his humble birth
  And Melancholy mark'd him for her own.

Large was his bounty, and his soul sincere;
  Heav'n did a recompense as largely send:
He gave to Mis'ry all he had, a tear,
  He gain'd from Heav'n ('twas all he wish'd) a
    friend.

No farther seek his merits to disclose,
  Or draw his frailties from their dread abode.
(There they alike in trembling hope repose,)
  The bosom of his Father and his God.

THOMAS GRAY

Richard Cory

Whenever Richard Cory went down town,
　　We people on the pavement looked at him;
He was a gentleman from sole to crown,
　　Clean favored, and imperially slim.

And he was always quietly arrayed,
　　And he was always human when he talked;
But still he fluttered pulses when he said,
　　"Good-morning," and he glittered when he
　　　　walked.

And he was rich—yes, richer than a king—
　　And admirably schooled in every grace:
In fine, we thought that he was everything
　　To make us wish that we were in his place.

So on we worked, and waited for the light,
　　And went without the meat, and cursed the bread;
And Richard Cory, one calm summer night,
　　Went home and put a bullet through his head.

EDWIN ARLINGTON ROBINSON

The Garden of Proserpine

Here, where the world is quiet;
  Here, where all trouble seems
Dead winds' and spent waves' riot
  In doubtful dreams of dreams
I watch the green field growing
For reaping folk and sowing,
For harvest-time and mowing,
  A sleepy world of streams.

I am tired of tears and laughter,
  And men that laugh and weep;
Of what may come hereafter
  For men that sow to reap:
I am weary of days and hours,
Blown buds of barren flowers,
Desires and dreams and powers
  And everything but sleep.

Here life has death for neighbor,
  And far from eye or ear
Wan waves and wet winds labor,
  Weak ships and spirits steer;
They drive adrift, and whither
They wot not who make thither;
But no such winds blow hither,
  And no such things grow here.

No growth of moor or coppice,
  No heather-flower or vine,
But bloomless buds of poppies,
  Green grapes of Proserpine,
Pale beds of blowing rushes,
Where no leaf blooms or blushes
Save this whereout she crushes
  For dead men deadly wine.

Pale, without name or number,
  In fruitless fields of corn,
They bow themselves and slumber
  All night till light is born;
And like a soul belated,
In hell and haven unmated,
By cloud and mist abated
  Comes out of darkness morn.

Though one were strong as seven,
  He too with death shall dwell,
Nor wake with wings in heaven,
  Nor weep for pains in hell;
Though one were fair as roses,
His beauty clouds and closes;
And well though love reposes,
  In the end it is not well.

Pale, beyond porch and portal,
   Crowned with calm leaves, she stands
Who gathers all things mortal
   With cold immortal hands;
Her languid lips are sweeter
Than love's who fears to greet her,
To men that mix and meet her
   From many times and lands.

She waits for each and other,
   She waits for all men born;
Forgets the earth her mother,
   The life of fruits and corn;
And spring and seed and swallow
Take wing for her and follow
Where summer song rings hollow
   And flowers are put to scorn.

There go the loves that wither,
   The old loves with wearier wings;
And all dead years draw thither,
   And all disastrous things;
Dead dreams of days forsaken,
Blind buds that snows have shaken,
Wild leaves that winds have taken,
   Red strays of ruined springs.

We are not sure of sorrow;
    And joy was never sure;
To-day will die to-morrow;
    Time stoops to no man's lure,
And love, grown faint and fretful,
With lips but half regretful
Sighs, and with eyes forgetful
    Weeps that no loves endure.

From too much love of living,
    From hope and fear set free,
We thank with brief thanksgiving
    Whatever gods may be
That no life lives for ever;
That dead men rise up never;
That even the weariest river
    Winds somewhere safe to sea.

Then star nor sun shall waken,
    Nor any change of light:
Nor sound of waters shaken,
    Nor any sound or sight:
Nor wintry leaves nor vernal,
Nor days nor things diurnal;
Only the sleep eternal
    In an eternal night.

ALGERNON CHARLES SWINBURNE

On File

If an unkind word appears,
   File the thing away.
If some novelty in jeers,
   File the thing away.
If some clever little bit
Of a sharp and pointed wit,
Carrying a sting with it—
   File the thing away.

If some bit of gossip come,
   File the thing away.
Scandalously spicy crumb,
   File the thing away.
If suspicion comes to you
That your neighbor isn't true
Let me tell you what to do—
   File the thing away.

Do this for a little while,
Then go out and burn the file.

JOHN KENDRICK BANGS

Dover Beach

The sea is calm to-night.
The tide is full, the moon lies fair
Upon the straits;—on the French coast the light
Gleams and is gone; the cliffs of England stand
Glimmering and vast, out in the tranquil bay.

Come to the window, sweet is the night-air!
Only, from the long line of spray
Where the sea meets the moon-blanch'd land,
Listen! you hear the grating roar
Of pebbles which the waves draw back, and fling,
At their return, up the high strand,
Begin, and cease, and then again begin,
With tremulous cadence slow, and bring
The eternal note of sadness in.

Sophocles long ago
Heard it on the Aegean, and it brought
Into his mind the turbid ebb and flow,
Of human misery; we
Find also in the sound a thought,
Hearing it by this distant northern sea.

The Sea of Faith
Was once, too, at the full, and round earth's shore
Lay like the folds of a bright girdle furl'd.
But now I only hear
Its melancholy, long, withdrawing roar,
Retreating, to the breath
Of the night-wind, down the vast edges drear
And naked shingles of the world.

Ah, love, let us be true
To one another! for the world, which seems
To lie before us like a land of dreams,
So various, so beautiful, so new,
Hath really neither joy, nor love, nor light,
Nor certitude, nor peace, nor help for pain;
And we are here as on a darkling plain
Swept with confused alarms of struggle and flight,
Where ignorant armies clash by night.

MATTHEW ARNOLD

REMEMBRANCE

With Rue My Heart Is Laden

With rue my heart is laden
    For golden friends I had,
For many a rose-lipt maiden
    And many a lightfoot lad.

By brooks too broad for leaping
    The lightfoot boys are laid;
The rose-lipt girls are sleeping
    In fields where roses fade.

A.E. HOUSMAN

John Anderson, My Jo

John Anderson, my jo, John,
  When we were first acquent;
Your locks were like the raven,
  Your bonnie brow was brent;[1]
But now your brow is bald, John,
  Your locks are like the snow;
But blessings on your frosty pow,[2]
  John Anderson, my jo.

John Anderson, my jo, John,
  We clamb the hill thegither;
And mony a cantie[3] day, John,
  We've had wi' ane anither:
Now we maun totter down, John,
  And hand in hand we'll go,
And sleep thegither at the foot,
  John Anderson, my jo.

ROBERT BURNS

1. *bright*
2. *head*
3. *merry*

Daisy

Where the thistle lifts a purple crown
    Six foot out of the turf,
And the harebell shakes on the windy hill—
    O the breath of the distant surf!—

The hills look over on the South,
    And southward dreams the sea;
And, with the sea-breeze hand in hand,
    Came innocence and she.

Where 'mid the gorse the raspberry
    Red for the gatherer springs,
Two children did we stray and talk
    Wise, idle, childish things.

She listen'd with big-lipp'd surprise,
    Breast-deep 'mid flower and spine:
Her skin was like a grape, whose veins
    Run snow instead of wine.

She knew not those sweet words she spake,
    Nor knew her own sweet way;
But there's never a bird, so sweet a song
    Throng'd in whose throat that day!

O, there were flowers in Storrington
        On the turf and on the spray;
But the sweetest flower on Sussex hills
        Was the Daisy-flower that day!

Her beauty smooth'd earth's furrow'd face!
        She gave me tokens three:—
A look, a word of her winsome mouth,
        And a wild raspberry.

A berry red, a guileless look,
        A still word,—strings of sand!
And yet they made my wild, wild heart
        Fly down to her little hand.

For, standing artless as the air,
        And candid as the skies,
She took the berries with her hand,
        And the love with her sweet eyes.

The fairest things have fleetest end:
        Their scent survives their close,
But the rose's scent is bitterness
        To him that loved the rose!

She looked a little wistfully,
   Then went her sunshine way:—
The sea's eye had a mist on it,
   And the leaves fell from the day.

She went her unremembering way,
   She went, and left in me
The pang of all the partings gone,
   And partings yet to be.

She left me marvelling why my soul
   Was sad that she was glad;
At all the sadness in the sweet,
   The sweetness in the sad.

Still, still I seem'd to see her, still
   Look up with soft replies,
And take the berries with her hand,
   And the love with her lovely eyes.

Nothing begins, and nothing ends,
   That is not paid with moan;
For we are born in other's pain,
   And perish in our own.

FRANCIS THOMPSON

I Remember, I Remember

I remember, I remember,
    The house where I was born,
The little window where the sun
    Came peeping in at morn:
He never came a wink too soon,
    Nor brought too long a day;
But now, I often wish the night
    Had borne my breath away.

I remember, I remember,
    The roses, red and white;
The violets and the lily-cups,
    Those flowers made of light!
The lilacs where the robin built,
    And where my brother set
The laburnum on his birthday,—
    The tree is living yet!

I remember, I remember,
　　Where I was used to swing;
And thought the air must rush as fresh
　　To swallows on the wing:
My spirit flew in feathers then,
　　That is so heavy now,
And summer pools could hardly cool
　　The fever on my brow!

I remember, I remember,
　　The fir trees dark and high;
I used to think their slender tops
　　Were close against the sky:
It was a childish ignorance,
　　But now 'tis little joy
To know I'm farther off from heaven
　　Than when I was a boy.

THOMAS HOOD

Ben Bolt

Don't you remember sweet Alice, Ben Bolt,—
　　Sweet Alice whose hair was so brown,
Who wept with delight when you gave her a smile,
　　And trembled with fear at your frown?
In the old churchyard in the valley, Ben Bolt,
　　In a corner obscure and alone,
They have fitted a slab of the granite so gray,
　　And Alice lies under the stone.

And don't you remember the school, Ben Bolt,
　　With the master so cruel and grim,
And the shaded nook in the running brook
　　Where the children went to swim?
Grass grows on the master's grave, Ben Bolt,
　　The spring of the brook is dry,
And of all the boys who were schoolmates then
　　There are only you and I.

THOMAS DUNN ENGLISH

Woodman, Spare that Tree

Woodman, spare that tree!
    Touch not a single bough!
In youth it sheltered me,
    And I'll protect it now.
'Twas my forefather's hand
    That placed it near his cot;
There, woodman, let it stand,
    Thy axe shall harm it not!

That old familiar tree,
    Whose glory and renown
Are spread o'er land and sea,
    And wouldst thou hew it down?
Woodman, forbear thy stroke!
    Cut not its earth-bound ties;
O, spare that aged oak,
    Now towering to the skies!

When but an idle boy
    I sought its grateful shade;
In all their gushing joy
    Here too my sisters played.
My mother kissed me here;
    My father pressed my hand—
Forgive this foolish tear,
    But let that old oak stand!

My heart-strings round thee cling,
    Close as thy bark, old friend!
Here shall the wild-bird sing,
    And still thy branches bend.
Old tree! the storm still brave!
    And, woodman, leave the spot;
While I've a hand to save,
    Thy axe shall hurt it not.

GEORGE PERKINS MORRIS

The Fly

Little Fly,
Thy summer's play
My thoughtless hand
Has brushed away.

Am not I
A fly like thee?
Or art not thou
A man like me?

For I dance
And drink and sing,
Till some blind hand
Shall brush my wing.

If thought is life
And strength and breath,
And the want
Of thought is death,

Then am I
A happy fly
If I live
Or if I die.

WILLIAM BLAKE

Auguries of Innocence

To see a world in a grain of sand
And a Heaven in a wild flower,
Hold Infinity in the palm of your hand
And Eternity in an hour.

A robin redbreast in a cage
Puts all Heaven in a rage.
A dove-house filled with doves and pigeons
Shudders Hell through all its regions.
A dog starved at his master's gate
Predicts the ruin of the state.
A horse misused upon the road
Calls to Heaven for human blood.

Each outcry of the hunted hare
A fibre from the brain does tear.
A skylark wounded in the wing,
A cherubim does cease to sing.
The game cock clipped and armed for fight
Does the rising sun affright.
Every wolf's and lion's howl
Raises from Hell a human soul.

The wild deer wandering here and there
Keeps the human soul from care.
The lamb misused breeds public strife
And yet forgives the butcher's knife.
The bat that flits at close of eve
Has left the brain that won't believe.
The owl that calls upon the night
Speaks the unbeliever's fright.

He who shall hurt the little wren
Shall never be beloved by men.
He who the ox to wrath had moved
Shall never be by woman loved.

The wanton boy that kills the fly
Shall feel the spider's enmity.
He who torments the chafer's sprite
Weaves a bower in endless night.

The caterpillar on the leaf
Repeats to thee thy mother's grief.
Kill not the moth nor butterfly
For the Last Judgment draweth nigh.

WILLIAM BLAKE

ROMANCE

Delight in Disorder

A sweet disorder in the dress
Kindles in clothes a wantonness:
A lawn about the shoulders thrown
Into a fine distraction,
An erring lace, which here and there
Enthralls the crimson stomacher,
A cuff neglectful, and thereby
Ribbands to flow confusedly,
A winning wave (deserving note)
In the tempestuous petticoat,
A careless shoe-string, in whose tie
I see a wild civility,
Do more bewitch me, than when art
Is too precise in every part.

ROBERT HERRICK

What Care I

Shall I, wasting in despair,
Die because a woman's fair?
Or my cheeks make pale with care
'Cause another's rosy are?
Be she fairer than the day
Or the flowery meads in May—
    If she be not so to me,
    What care I how fair she be?

Great or good, or kind or fair,
I will ne'er the more despair;
If she love me, this believe,
I will die ere she shall grieve;

If she slight me when I woo,
I can scorn and let her go.
    For if she be not for me,
    What care I for whom she be?

GEORGE WITHER

What My Lover Said

By the merest chance, in the twilight gloom,
    In the orchard path he met me;
In the tall, wet grass, with its faint perfume,
And I tried to pass, but he made no room,
    Oh, I tried, but he would not let me.
So I stood and blushed till the grass grew red,
    With my face bent down above it,
While he took my hand as he whispering said—
(How the clover lifted each pink, sweet head,
To listen to all that my lover said;
    Oh, the clover in bloom, I love it!)

In the high, wet grass went the path to hide,
    And the low, wet leaves hung over;
But I could not pass upon either side,
For I found myself, when I vainly tried,
    In the arms of my steadfast lover.
And he held me there and he raised my head,
    While he closed the path before me,
And he looked down into my eyes and said—
(How the leaves bent down from the boughs
      o'er head,
To listen to all that my lover said;
    Oh, the leaves hanging lowly o'er me!)

Had he moved aside but a litle way,
    I could surely then have passed him;
And he knew I never could wish to stay,
And would not have heard what he had to say,
    Could I only aside have cast him.
It was almost dark, and the moments sped,
    And the searching night wind found us,
But he drew me nearer and softly said—
(How the pure, sweet wind grew still, instead,
To listen to all that my lover said;
    Oh, the whispering wind around us!)

I know that the grass and the leaves will not tell,
    And I'm sure that the wind, precious rover,
Will carry my secret so safely and well
    That no being shall ever discover

One word of the many that rapidly fell
    From the soul-speaking lips of my lover;
    And from the moon and the stars that looked over
Shall never reveal what a fairy-like spell
They wove round about us that night in the dell,
    In the path through the dew-laden clover,
Nor echo the whispers that made my heart swell
    As they fell from the lips of my lover.

HOMER   GREENE

The Highwayman

Part One

The wind was a torrent of darkness among the gusty
    trees,
The moon was a ghostly galleon tossed upon cloudy
    seas,
The road was a ribbon of moonlight over the purple
    moor,
And the highwayman came riding—
    Riding—riding—
The highwayman came riding, up to the old inn-door.

He'd a French cocked-hat on his forehead, a bunch of
    lace at his chin,
A coat of claret velvet, and breeches of brown
    doeskin:
They fitted with never a wrinkle; his boots were up to
    the thigh!
And he rode with a jewelled twinkle,
    His pistol butts a-twinkle,
His rapier hilt a-twinkle, under the jewelled sky.

Over the cobbles he clattered and clashed in the dark
      inn-yard,
And he tapped with his whip on the shutters, but all
      was locked and barred:
He whistled a tune to the window, and who should be
      waiting there
But the landlord's black-eyed daughter,
    Bess, the landlord's daughter,
Plaiting a dark red love-knot into her long black hair.

And then in the dark old inn-yard a stable-wicket
      creaked
Where Tim, the ostler, listened; his face was white
      and peaked,
His eyes were hollows of madness, his hair like moldy
      hay;
But he loved the landlord's daughter,
    The landlord's red-lipped daughter:
Dumb as a dog he listened, and he heard the robber
      say—

"One kiss, my bonny sweetheart, I'm after a prize
      tonight,
But I shall be back with the yellow gold before the
      morning light.
Yet if they press me sharply, and harry me through
      the day,

Then look for me by moonlight,
    Watch for me by moonlight:
I'll come to thee by moonlight, though Hell should
        bar the way."

He rose upright in the stirrups, he scarce could reach
        her hand;
But she loosened her hair i' the casement! His face
        burnt like a brand
As the black cascade of perfume came tumbling over
        his breast;
And he kissed its waves in the moonlight,
    (Oh, sweet black waves in the moonlight)
Then he tugged at his reins in the moonlight, and
        galloped away to the West.

Part Two

He did not come in the dawning; he did not come at
        noon;
And out of the tawny sunset, before the rise o' the
        moon,
When the road was a gypsy's ribbon, looping the pur-
        ple moor,
A red-coat-troop came marching—
    Marching—marching—
King George's men came marching, up to the old inn-
        door.

They said no word to the landlord, they drank his ale
      instead;
But they gagged his daughter and bound her to the
      foot of her narrow bed.
Two of them knelt at her casement, with muskets at
      the side!
There was death at every window;
   And Hell at one dark window;
For Bess could see, through her casement, the road
      that *he* would ride.

They had tied her up to attention, with many a snig-
      gering jest:
They had bound a musket beside her, with the barrel
      beneath her breast!
"Now keep good watch!" and they kissed her.
   She heard the dead man say—
Look for me by moonlight;
   Watch for me by moonlight;
I'll come to thee by moonlight, though Hell should
      bar the way!

She twisted her hands behind her; but all the knots
      held good!
She writhed her hands till her fingers were wet with
      sweat or blood!
They stretched and strained in the darkness, and the
      hours crawled by like years;

Till, now, on the stroke of midnight,
  Cold, on the stroke of midnight,
The tip of one finger touched it! The trigger at least
    was hers!

The tip of one finger touched it; she strove no more
    for the rest!
Up, she stood up to attention, with the barrel beneath
    her breast,
She would not risk their hearing: she would not strive
    again;
For the road lay bare in the moonlight,
  Blank and bare in the moonlight;
And the blood of her veins in the moonlight throbbed
    to her Love's refrain.

Tlot-tlot, tlot-tlot! Had they heard it? The horse-hoofs
    ringing clear—
Tlot-tlot, tlot-tlot, in the distance? Were they deaf
    that they did not hear?
Down the ribbon of moonlight, over the brow of the
    hill,
The highwayman came riding,
  Riding, riding!
The red-coats looked to their priming! She stood up
    straight and still!

Tlot-tlot, in the frosty silence; *Tlot-tlot* in the echoing
    night!
Nearer he came and nearer! Her face was like a light!
Her eyes grew wide for a moment; she drew one last
    deep breath,
Then her finger moved in the moonlight,
    Her musket shattered the moonlight,
Shattered her breast in the moonlight and warned
    him—with her death.

He turned; he spurred him Westward; he did not
    know who stood
Bowed with her head o'er the musket, drenched with
    her own red blood!
Not till the dawn he heard it, and slowly blanched to
    hear
How Bess, the landlord's daughter,
    The landlord's black-eyed daughter,
Had watched for her Love in the moonlight; and died
    in the darkness there.

Back, he spurred like a madman, shrieking a curse to
    the sky,
With the white road smoking behind him, and his
    rapier brandished high!
Blood-red were his spurs i' the golden noon; wine-red
    was his velvet coat;

When they shot him down on the highway,
   Down like a dog on the highway,
And he lay in his blood on the highway, with the
      bunch of lace at his throat.

And still a winter's night, they say, when the wind is
      in the trees,
When the moon is a ghostly galleon tossed upon
      cloudy seas,
When the road is a ribbon of moonlight over the pur-
      ple moor,
A highwayman comes riding—
   Riding—riding—
A highwayman comes riding, up to the old inn-door.

Over the cobbles he clatters and clangs in the dark
      inn-yard;
And he taps with his whip on the shutters, but all is
      locked and barred:
He whistles a tune to the window, and who should be
      waiting there
But the landlord's black-eyed daughter,
   Bess, the landlord's daughter,
Plaiting a dark red love-knot into her long black hair.

ALFRED NOYES

Why So Pale and Wan

Why so pale and wan, fond lover?
    Prithee, why so pale?
Will, when looking well can't move her,
    Looking ill prevail?
    Prithee, why so pale?

Why so dull and mute, young sinner?
    Prithee, why so mute?
Will, when speaking well can't win her,
    Saying nothing do 't?
    Prithee, why so mute?

Quit, quit for shame! This will not move;
    This cannot take her.
If of herself she will not love,
    Nothing can make her.
    The devil take her!

SIR JOHN SUCKLING

Tell Her So

Amid the cares of married strife
   In spite of toil and business life
If you value your dear wife—
   Tell her so!

When days are dark and deeply blue
   She has her troubles, same as you
Show her that your love is true
   Tell her so!

Whether you mean or care,
Gentleness, kindness, love, and hate,
Envy, anger, are there.
Then, would you quarrels avoid
And peace and love rejoice?
Keep anger not only out of your words—
Keep it out of your voice.

AUTHOR UNKNOWN

If We Knew

If we knew the woe and heartache
    Waiting for us down the road,
If our lips could taste the wormwood,
    If our backs could feel the load,
Would we waste the day in wishing
    For a time that ne'er can be?
Would we wait in such impatience
    For our ships to come from sea?

If we knew the baby fingers
    Pressed against the windowpane
Would be cold and stiff tomorrow—
    Never trouble us again—
Would the bright eyes of our darling
    Catch the frown upon our brow?
Would the print of rosy fingers
    Vex us then as they do now?

Ah! these little ice-cold fingers—
    How they point our memories back
To the hasty words and actions
    Strewn along our backward track!
How these little hands remind us,
    As in snowy grace they lie,
Not to scatter thorns—but roses—
    For our reaping by and by.

Strange we never prize the music
    Till the sweet-voiced bird has flown;
Strange that we should slight the violets
    Till the lovely flowers are gone;
Strange that summer skies and sunshine
    Never seem one half so fair
As when winter's snowy pinions
    Shake their white down in the air!

Lips from which the seal of silence
    None but God can roll away,
Never blossomed in such beauty
    As adorns the mouth today;
And sweet words that freight our memory
    With their beautiful perfume,
Come to us in sweeter accents
    Through the portals of the tomb.

Let us gather up the sunbeams
    Lying all around our path;
Let us keep the wheat and roses,
    Casting out the thorns and chaff;
Let us find our sweetest comfort
    In the blessings of today,
With a patient hand removing
    All the briars from the way.

MAY RILEY SMITH

Those We Love the Best

One great truth in life I've found,
    While journeying to the West—
The only folks we really wound
    Are those we love the best.

The man you thoroughly despise
    Can rouse your wrath, 'tis true;
Annoyance in your heart will rise
    At things mere strangers do.

But those are only passing ills;
    This rule all lives will prove;
The rankling wound which aches and thrills
    Is dealt by hands we love.

The choicest garb, the sweetest grace,
    Are oft to strangers shown;
The careless mien, the frowning face,
    Are given to our own.

We flatter those we scarcely know,
    We please the fleeting guest,
And deal full many a thoughtless blow
    To those we love the best. . . .

ELLA WHEELER WILCOX

The Sin of Omission

It isn't the thing you do;
    It's the thing you leave undone,
Which gives you a bit of heartache
    At the setting of the sun.

The tender word forgotten,
    The letter you did not write,
The flower you might have sent,
    Are your haunting ghosts tonight.

The stone you might have lifted
    Out of a brother's way,
The bit of heartsome counsel
    You were hurried too much to say.

The loving touch of the hand,
    The gentle and winsome tone,
That you had no time or thought for
    With troubles enough of your own.

The little acts of kindness,
   So easily out of mind;
Those chances to be helpful
   Which everyone may find—

No, it's not the thing you do,
   It's the thing you leave undone,
Which gives you the bit of heartache
   At the setting of the sun.

MARGARET E. SANGSTER

Our Own

If I had known in the morning
    How wearily all the day
The words unkind would trouble my mind
    That I said when you went away,
I had been more careful, darling,
    Nor given you needless pain;
But we vex our own with look and tone
    We may never take back again.

For though in the quiet evening
    You may give me the kiss of peace,
Yet it well might be that never for me
    The pain of the heart should cease!
How many go forth at morning
    Who never come home at night!
And hearts have broken for harsh words spoken
    That sorrow can ne'er set right.

We have careful thought for the stranger,
    And smiles for the sometime guest;
But oft for "our own" the bitter tone,
    Though we love our own the best.
Ah! lips with the curve impatient,
    Ah! brow with the shade of scorn,
'Twere a cruel fate, were the night too late
    To undo the work of the morn!

MARGARET E. SANGSTER

If I Had Known

If I had known what trouble you were bearing;
What griefs were in the silence of your face;
I would have been more gentle, and more caring,
And tried to give you gladness for a space.
I would have brought more warmth into the place,
    If I had known.

If I had known what thoughts despairing drew you;
(Why do we never try to understand?)
I would have lent a little friendship to you,
And slipped my hand within your hand,
And made you stay more pleasant in the land,
    If I had known.

MARY CAROLYN DAVIES

To Youth

This I say to you:
Be arrogant! Be true!
True to April's lust that sings
Through your veins. These sharp Springs
Matter most . . . After years
Will be time enough to sleep . . .
Carefulness . . . and tears . . .

Now while life is raw and new,
Drink it clear, drink it deep!
Let the moonlight's lunacy
Tear away your cautions.
Be proud, and mad, and young, and free!
Grasp a comet! Kick at stars
Laughingly! Fight! Dare!
Arms are soft, breasts are white.
Magic's in the April night—

Never fear, Age will catch you,
Slow you down, ere it dispatch you
To your long and solemn quiet . . .
What will matter—then—the riot
Of the lilacs in the wind?
What will mean—then—the crush
Of lips at hours when birds hush?
Purple, green and flame will end
In a calm, gray blend.

Only graven in your soul
After all the rest is gone
There will be ecstasies . . .
These alone . . .

JOHN WEAVER

How Old Are You?

Age is a quality of mind.
If you have left your dreams behind,
   If hope is cold,
If you no longer look ahead,
If your ambitions' fires are dead—
   Then you are old.

But if from life you take the best,
And if in life you keep the jest,
   If love you hold;
No matter how the years go by,
No matter how the birthdays fly—
   You are not old.

H.S. FRITSCH

When I Was One-and-Twenty

When I was one-and-twenty
    I heard a wise man say,
"Give crowns and pounds and guineas
    But not your heart away;
Give pearls away and rubies
    But keep your fancy free."
But I was one-and-twenty,
    No use to talk to me.

When I was one-and-twenty
    I heard him say again,
"The heart out of the bosom
    Was never given in vain;
'Tis paid with sighs a-plenty
    And sold for endless rue."
And I am two-and-twenty,
    And oh, 'tis true, 'tis true.

A.E. HOUSMAN

Growing Old

The days grow shorter, the nights grow longer;
   The headstones thicken along the way;
And life grows sadder, but love grows stronger
   For those who walk with us day by day.

The tear comes quicker, the laugh comes slower;
   The courage is lesser to do and dare;
And the tide of joy in the heart falls lower,
   And seldom covers the reefs of care.

But all true things in the world seem truer,
   And the better things of earth seem best,
And friends are dearer, as friends are fewer,
   And love is all as our sun dips west.

Then let us clasp hands as we walk together,
   And let us speak softly in low, sweet tone,
For no man knows on the morrow whether
   We two pass on—or but one alone.

ELLA WHEELER WILCOX

The New Colossus

Not like the brazen giant of Greek fame,
With conquering limbs astride from land to land;
Here at our sea-washed, sunset gates shall stand
A mighty woman with a torch, whose flame
Is the imprisoned lightning, and her name
Mother of Exiles. From her beacon-hand
Glows world-wide welcome; her mild eyes command
The air-bridged harbor that twin cities frame.

"Keep ancient lands, your storied pomp!" cries she
With silent lips. "Give me your tired, your poor,
Your huddled masses yearning to breathe free,
The wretched refuse of your teeming shore.
Send these, the homeless, tempest-tost to me,
I lift my lamp beside the golden door!"

EMMA LAZARUS

INDEX OF FIRST LINES

INDEX OF FIRST LINES

INDEX OF AUTHORS

INDEX OF AUTHORS

INDEX OF TITLES

INDEX OF TITLES

ACKNOWLEDGMENTS

ACKNOWLEDGMENTS

Thanks to the following publishers for their permission to reprint the poems listed:

ANTHEM FOR DOOMED YOUTH from *Collected Poems of Wilfred Owen*. Copyright Chatto and Windus Ltd., 1963. Reprinted by permission of New Directions Publishing Corporation.

CHICAGO from *Chicago Poems* by Carl Sandburg, copyright 1916 by Holt, Rinehart and Winston, Inc.; renewed 1944 by Carl Sandburg. Reprinted by permission of Harcourt Brace Jovanovich, Inc.

COOL TOMBS, and GRASS from *Cornhuskers* by Carl Sandburg. Copyright by 1918 by Holt, Rinehart and Winston, Inc.; renewed 1946 by Carl Sandburg. Reprinted by permission of Harcourt Brace Jovanovich, Inc.

DEATH IS A DOOR by Nancy Byrd Turner. Reprinted by permission of The Golden Quill Press.

FLEURETTE, and CARRY ON from *The Collected Poems of Robert Service*. Reprinted by permission of Dodd, Mead & Company, Inc. Copyright 1916 by Dodd, Mead & Company. Copyright renewed 1944 by Robert W. Service. Thanks to McGraw-Hill Ryerson Limited of Scarborough, Ontario, Canada for permission to reprint these poems in Canada.

HUSBAND AND WIFE, and WELCOME OVER THE DOOR OF AN OLD INN by Arthur Guiterman, with permission of Louise H. Sclove.

I HAVE A RENDEZVOUS WITH DEATH by Alan Seeger from *Poems*. Copyright 1916 by Charles Scribner's Sons; copyright renewed 1944 by Elsie Adams Seeger. Reprinted with the permission of Charles Scribner's Sons.

IN FLANDERS FIELDS from *In Flanders Fields and Other Poems* by John McCrae. Reprinted by permission of G. P. Putnam's Sons. Copyright 1919; renewed 1947 by John McCrae.

I SHALL NOT CARE from *Collected Poems of Sara Teasdale*. Reprinted with permission of Macmillan Publishing Co., Inc. Copyright 1915 by Macmillan Publishing Co., Inc., renewed 1943 by Mamie T. Wheless.

LEISURE, and MONEY copyright © 1963 by Jonathan Cape. Ltd. Reprinted from *The Complete Works of W. H. Davies* by permission of Wesleyan University Press. Thanks to Jonathan Cape Ltd. for permission to reprint these poems in Canada.

OF DE WITT WILLIAMS ON HIS WAY TO LINCOLN CEMETERY from *The World of Gwendolyn Brooks* by Gwendolyn Brooks. Copyright 1945 by Gwendolyn Brooks Blakely. Reprinted by permission of Harper & Row Publishers, Inc.

ON CHILDREN, ON FRIENDSHIP, ON LOVE, ON MARRIAGE reprinted from *The Prophet* by Kahlil Gibran, by permission of Alfred A. Knopf, Inc. Copyright 1923 by Kahlil Gibran and renewed 1951 by Administrators C.T.A. of Kahlil Gibran Estate, and Mary Gibran.

ONLY A DAD, FATHER, ON GOING HOME FOR CHRISTMAS, NO PLACE TO GO, HOME, THE JUNK BOX, PEOPLE LIKED HIM, DEFEAT, IT COULDN'T BE DONE from *The Collected Verse of Edgar Guest*, with permission of Contemporary Books, Inc.

PATTERNS from *The Complete Works of Amy Lowell*, by Amy Lowell. Copyright 1955 by Houghton Mifflin Company. Reprinted by permission of the publisher, Houghton Mifflin Company.

PRAYER by Louis Untermeyer. Copyright 1914 by Harcourt Brace Jovanovich, Inc.; renewed 1942 by Louis Untermeyer. Reprinted from *Long Feud: Selected Poems* by Louis Untermeyer by permission of Harcourt Brace Jovanovich, Inc.

PRAYER FOR THIS HOUSE from *This Singing World* by Louis Untermeyer. Copyright 1923 by Harcourt Brace Jovanovich, Inc.; renewed 1951 by Louis Untermeyer. Reprinted by permission of the publisher.

THE HOUSE ON THE HILL, and RICHARD CORY by Edwin Arlington Robinson from *The Children of the Night*. Copyright under the Berne Convention. Reprinted with the permission of Charles Scribner's Sons.

THE SOLDIER by Rupert Brooke, reprinted by permission of Dodd, Mead & Company, Inc., from *The Collected Poems of Rupert Brooke*. Copyright 1915 by Dodd, Mead & Company. Copyright renewed 1943 by Edward March.

TO YOUTH reprinted from *In American: The Collected Poems of John V.A. Weaver,* by John V.A. Weaver, by permission of Alfred A. Knopf, Inc., Copyright 1928 and renewed 1965 by Margaret Wood Walling.

TREES by Joyce Kilmer. Copyright 1913 and renewed 1941. Copyright assigned to Jerry Vogel Music Co., Inc., 58 West 45th Street, New York, N.Y. 10036. Used by permission of copyright owner. Reproduction prohibited.

WHEN I WAS ONE-AND-TWENTY, and WITH RUE MY HEART IS LADEN from "A Shropshire Lad"—Authorised Edition—from *The Collected Poems of A. E. Housman.* Copyright 1939, 1940, © 1965 by Holt Rinehart and Winston. Copyright © 1967, 1968 by Robert E. Symons. Thanks to the Society of Authors, London, England, for permission to reprint these poems in Canada.

WHAT LIPS MY LIPS HAVE KISSED from *Collected Poems,* Harper & Row. Copyright 1923, 1951 by Edna St. Vincent Millay and Norma Millay Ellis.

WHAT THOMAS AN BULIE SAID IN A PUB from *Collected Poems of James Stephens.* Reprinted with permission of Macmillan Publishing Co., Inc. Thanks to The Society of Authors, London, England, on behalf of the copyright owner, Mrs. Iris Wise, for permission to reprint this poem in Canada.

The following selections were reprinted with the permission of Hart Publishing Company from POEMS YOU'LL READ AGAIN AND AGAIN compiled by Harold H. Hart:

Henry Wadsworth Longfellow, "The Village Blacksmith"
Carl Sandburg, "Chicago"
Samuel Taylor Coleridge, "The Rime of the Ancient Mariner"
Ella Wheeler Wilcox, "I Love You"
Sara Teasdale, "I Shall Not Care"
Nellie Womach Hines, "Home"
William Shakespeare, "When in Disgrace with Fortune and Men's Eyes"
Wilbur D. Nesbit, "Who Hath a Book"
Edwin Arlington Robinson, "Richard Cory"
Emma Lazarus, "The New Colossus"

Diligent effort has been made to credit all the authors of the poems in this volume. Yet in some cases we have not succeeded in tracking down the address of the copyright owner or of the copyright owner's successor in interest. Where we have been unable to accord proper credit, forgiveness is implored.